Vietnam Today
A Guide to a Nation at a Crossroads

More early praise for Mark Ashwill and *Vietnam Today*

"*Vietnam Today* provides constructive advice to those who wish to build lasting relationships with their Vietnamese counterparts. Most importantly, *Vietnam Today* helps the reader understand enduring aspects of traditional culture in the context of a country undergoing profound and rapid change."
—Patti McGill Peterson, Executive Director,
International Exchange of Scholars

"Mark Ashwill has provided us with a primer that will help Americans and the world community understand the people, the culture, the history and the spirit of the Vietnamese. This is an important step in helping us understand an emerging country in the world community."
—Stephen T. Banko III, Vietnam War Veteran

"At last, an introduction to Vietnam that is about a country rather than a war. Ashwill and Diep have built a cultural bridge you will want to cross."
—Dr. Allan E. Goodman, President and CEO,
Institute of International Education

"*Vietnam Today* is a very balanced primer of history, culture and psychology. A must-read for anyone planning a business trip to Vietnam."
—P. Joseph Koessler, Former Strategic Marketing Manager,
Coca-Cola Southeast and West Asia Division

"With great interest, I read your book from cover to cover. I cried, I laughed, I smiled, my eyes full of silent tears as I read what you wrote. For the first time, I don't get annoyed with a 'foreigner' talking about my country and my people."
—Nguyen Phuong Mai, reporter,
Sinh Vien Viet Nam (Vietnam Student News)

Vietnam Today

A Guide to a Nation at a Crossroads

Mark A. Ashwill

with THAI NGOC DIEP

INTERCULTURAL PRESS
A Nicholas Brealey Publishing Company

YARMOUTH, ME • BOSTON • LONDON

First published by Intercultural Press, a Nicholas Brealey Publishing Company, in 2005

Intercultural Press, Inc.
A Nicholas Brealey Publishing Company
PO Box 700
Yarmouth, Maine 04096 USA
Tel: 207-846-5168
Fax: 207-846-5181
www.interculturalpress.com

Nicholas Brealey Publishing
3-5 Spafield Street, Clerkenwell
London, EC1R 4QB, UK

Tel: +44-(0)-207-239-0360
Fax: +44-(0)-207-239-0370
www.nbrealey-books.com

Printed in the United States of America

09 08 07 06 05   1 2 3 4 5

ISBN: 1-931930-09-0

Library of Congress Cataloging-in-Publication Data
   Ashwill, Mark A.
      Vietnam today : a guide to a nation at a crossroads / Mark A. Ashwill with Thai Ngoc Diep.—
   1st. ed.
         p. cm.
      Includes bibliographical references.
         ISBN 1-931930-09-0 (alk. paper)
      1. Vietnam.   2. Business etiquette—Vietnam.   I. Thai, Ngoc Diep, 1975–   II. Title.
         DS556.3.A74 2004
         959.704'4—dc22

                                                                              2004023585

Dedicated to those Vietnamese and foreigners who serve as bridges between their respective cultures and who work together in the name of peace, prosperity, and friendship

A thousand years of Chinese rule,
A hundred years of French subjugation,
And ten years of American domination,
But we survived, unified.

—Vietnamese saying

Contents

Acknowledgments

I owe a debt of gratitude to my collaborator and junior partner, Thai Ngoc Diep, who assisted me with *Vietnam Today*. (See her biographical sketch in "To the Reader.") Without her this project would not have come to fruition. My heartfelt thanks also go to Judy Carl-Hendrick, managing editor of Intercultural Press, for working her magic, and to Patricia O'Hare, publisher of Intercultural Press, for her support.

I wish to acknowledge the contribution of Lady Borton, whom I met for the first time last year in Hanoi. Like the Vietnamese among whom she lives, Lady (her real name) is a modest woman who would no doubt blush at hearing me say that she is something of a living legend in Vietnam. (It has been said that she is a Vietnamese disguised as a U.S. American, high praise indeed.) She came to Quang Ngai province to work in a Quaker Service rehabilitation center for civilian amputees from 1969 to 1971. Since then, she has devoted much of her career and life to Vietnam. Lady is the country representative for the American Friends Service Committee (Quaker Service) in Hanoi.

Lady's unpublished essay, "To Be Sure . . . : Work Practices in Viet Nam," parts of which I have used and cited in *Vietnam Today* and which I list as a recommended reading, contains information about cultural dimensions, work practices, and relationship building, as well as principles for working in Vietnam. Much of the analysis and advice contained in this widely circulated work, which is well known within the expat community and among foreigners who travel to Vietnam on a regular basis, was affirmed by our Vietnamese and expatriate respondents. Lady is an inspiration to me and many others, and a treasure trove of information about Vietnamese culture and society.

It is with deep gratitude and joy that I acknowledge the many individuals and institutions in Vietnam and the United States that helped make this book possible. They include the Council for International Exchange of Scholars (CIES), which enabled me to work in 2003 as a visiting scholar in Hanoi under the auspices of a Fulbright Senior Specialists Grant; United University Professions (UUP), for professional development grants that allowed me to continue my Vietnam-related work; the U.S.-Indochina Educational Foundation, Inc. (USIEF), the State University of New York at Buffalo (SUNY/Buffalo), and the many Vietnamese nationals and expatriates from Australia, France, Germany, the U.S., the UK, and other countries who set aside precious time to share with us their knowledge, experience, wisdom and advice in the form of completed surveys, interviews, e-mail exchanges, and telephone conversations.

I am grateful to Le Minh Ngoc, Nguyen Phuong Mai, and Pham Thi Hong Van, who read and commented on various drafts of *Vietnam Today* with great care and insight. They gladly played the roles of sounding board, cultural informant, and critic. I would also like to thank Pham Minh Hang, who has been a steadfast source of support and inspiration. There are unnamed others who contributed to this project in ways both tangible and intangible. They, too, have my gratitude.

Thanks to Professor Huu Ngoc, a renowned Vietnamese writer, journalist, and translator, who was generous enough to spend some time with me on a cool, rainy May morning in his office at The Gio Publishers in Hanoi. A prolific writer and lecturer who has traveled extensively, Professor Ngoc has been described as a "span of the cultural bridge joining Vietnam to other cultures."

Vietnam Today is, in some respects, a collective work. It contains the advice, ideas, experiences and reflections of people far more experienced than Thai Ngoc Diep or I. However, neither these individuals nor those mentioned above can be held responsible for errors of omission or commission that may be found herein. Any shortcomings in the substance and content of this book are our sole responsibility.

Mark A. Ashwill
Buffalo, New York, USA
Hanoi, Vietnam

To the Reader

In my personal and professional life, I have had the opportunity and privilege to become acquainted with two countries that shared the world stage in the twentieth century and whose fates have been interwoven— for better and for worse—with that of my country, the United States of America. In one, the Federal Republic of Germany, the vanquished became a cherished ally and key player in the postwar world order. In the other, the Socialist Republic of Vietnam, the victor remained a hated enemy, became an obsession, and insinuated itself into the national psyche, pervading the popular culture of the U.S. and forever transforming that nation's political discourse.

In Germany, I learned the language, studied, taught, and conducted research. In Vietnam, I have developed programs for students and businesspeople, have worked under the auspices of a Fulbright Senior Specialists Grant, and have just begun to scratch the surface of a beautiful and expressive language that has no fewer than six tones. Each visit has been a profound learning experience and an inspiration to delve ever deeper into Vietnamese culture, to learn from others far more experienced and knowledgeable than I, and to share that information and knowledge through articles, conversations, lectures, workshops, and now *Vietnam Today: A Guide to a Nation at a Crossroads*.

I vividly recall my first trip to Vietnam in January 1996. Looking at the coastline, jungle, and rice paddies below, I thought of the grisly televised images I had come to know as a child growing up in the 1960s. As someone who came of age as the war was winding down, I rejoiced at the prospect of visiting a Vietnam at peace. With each return visit, including several in 2003 and 2004, this sense of excitement, joy, and hope has yet to lose any of its initial intensity.

Thai Ngoc Diep assisted me in researching *Vietnam Today*. Thai was born in 1975, the year the war ended and Vietnam was reunited. She received her B.A. in International Business from the Hanoi Foreign Trade University and her M.A. in International Business and World Trade from the State University of New York at Buffalo. Before pursuing graduate study in the United States, Thai worked for the Hanoi offices of the U.S.-Vietnam Trade Council, an American nonprofit organization dedicated to promoting trade between the U.S. and Vietnam, and for Ericcson, a Swedish company that is one of the world's leading manufacturers of consumer communications and data products.

Thai's perspective is that of a bilingual and bicultural Vietnamese woman who has had extensive experience with U.S. Americans and other Westerners in business and academic settings. This includes individuals who were unsuccessful because they tried in vain to make the Vietnamese fit into their narrow cultural framework, as well as others who listened, watched, and learned how to negotiate their way successfully through Vietnamese culture, learning from both negative and positive role models. Thai and other members of the postwar generation grew up in a time of deprivation and uncertainty, but also of hope, optimism, and increasing material well-being. Witnesses to and participants in a transformation of historic proportions, they are the future of Vietnam.

Together, we bring a multitude of perspectives and experiences to bear on the increasingly popular and practical subject of Vietnam as a country. We are fortunate to be able to play a small role, mainly as academics, nonprofit workers, and "citizen diplomats," in shaping the future relationship of our countries. Our different and at times divergent perspectives have served as a system of checks and balances, making for a richer and more in-depth survey of Vietnamese behavioral culture. In some respects, writing this book has been a process of converting theory into practice, especially as it relates to work and communication styles.

Thai and I share a passionate desire to inform our readers about the sources of misunderstanding between Vietnam, the U.S., and other Western countries, and to explore and suggest ways in which these often sizable gaps can be bridged. For foreigners who have done their homework and gauged their expectations to reality, Vietnam can be a land of opportunity. If you plan to travel to Vietnam, success is within reach if you bring along the type of basic knowledge of Vietnamese culture that you will find in *Vietnam Today*—as well as a long-term perspective, a schedule and budget that allow for regular trips to Vietnam, and renewable reserves of energy and perseverance.

The U.S. and Vietnam have a special relationship, born of bloodshed and redeemed in peaceful, productive, and mutually beneficial interaction. This is what President Bill Clinton meant during his historic November 2000 visit to Vietnam when he spoke of how "the histories of our two nations are deeply intertwined in ways that are both a source of pain for generations that came before and a source of promise for generations yet to come." This statement, as eloquent as it is accurate, resonates on an intellectual, emotional, and spiritual level. Indeed, it is the perfect embodiment of the spirit in which *Vietnam Today* is written.

As educators and practitioners, we owe it to you, our readers, to tell you the truth not only about "Vietnam" as a war but also, more important, about Vietnam as a dynamic, beautiful, and captivating country that, for all of its problems, is at peace, without foreign occupation and with a promising future. Working in Vietnam can be an exhilarating experience that will test your mettle and, at times, push you to the limit. But if you are sufficiently well prepared, have a temperament that embraces flexibility and patience, and are willing to adopt a long-term view of the concept of "return on investment"—whatever that investment may be—then your chances of success will increase considerably.

Mark A. Ashwill
Buffalo, New York, USA
Hanoi, Vietnam

Introduction

Vietnam gives you space to challenge all of your ideas and all of the assumptions that you inherit growing up in the West—not necessarily to reject but to explore them, to see whether they are actually valid, or one alternative way of understanding the world.

—Australian NGO manager

I think Vietnamese characteristics can be described like the seven colors of rainbow: the green of courtesy, the blue of peace, the yellow of warmth, the orange of enthusiasm, the red of confidence, the purple of loyalty and the indigo of intellect.

—Mai Vy, student

Vietnam is an intriguing and harmonious blend of the ancient and the modern, from symbols of war and suffering neighbors to monuments of the new market economy. You can stroll through Lenin Park (yes, *that* Lenin) in distinctly capitalist Hanoi for a retreat from the never-ending stream of traffic, and see for yourself what urban Vietnamese do for recreation and health. Or visit the Hoa Lo Prison, better known to the rest of the world as the "Hanoi Hilton," originally built by the French to imprison Viet Minh fighters and later used to hold U.S. Navy pilots, one

of whom would later become and the first U.S. ambassador to the Socialist Republic of Vietnam, who were shot down over northern Vietnam.
Most of the sprawling compound was demolished to make way for an
office building, a luxury hotel, apartments, and upscale shops during
Hanoi's building boom of the late 1990s. What remains is a museum, a
"must-see" tourist attraction that spans two periods of Vietnamese
history.

Next, you can sit across the street in a popular Internet café—a sign
of the times—side by side with young Vietnamese, cold drink in hand,
exchanging e-mails with friends around the world, chatting online, or
searching websites for scholarship opportunities that might allow them
to fulfill their dream of study abroad. The information age has arrived in
Vietnam in full force, with small shops advertising "Internet, E-mail,
WWW, Chat" for 50 cents or less per hour.

Walk around Hanoi on a sultry summer night and experience a cele-
bration of life: horns honking, motorbikes flowing like water around
pedestrians at breakneck speed, lovers sitting on park benches wrapped
in each other's arms, older people exercising, children playing bad-
minton, vendors plying their trade—the wars and colonial violence that
beset this country for so many generations a distant and fading memory.
Or enjoy a leisurely dinner with friends on the streets of Ho Chi Minh
City (HCM City), formerly Saigon, and delight in the cool breeze that is
a rewarding end to a scorching day in this, the more tropical region of the
country.

As a diplomat with significant Vietnam experience once told me, one
must be a marathon runner, not a sprinter, in order to be successful in
Vietnam. Sometimes the pace is excruciatingly slow; at times, however,
good things can happen at the speed of light. In another wise piece of
advice, a partner in a multinational firm told me bluntly, "Vietnam is not
the place to be if you're not willing to lose money." Another expat with
years of Vietnam experience advised: "Patience and perseverance will get
you a long way here. Don't come feeling you are going to 'save' anyone."
With few exceptions—and the gold rush mentality of the 1990s notwith-

standing—Vietnam is not a place where get-rich-quick schemes are likely to succeed.

Why do foreigners come to Vietnam—not the millions who visit as tourists every year—but those who come to live or otherwise make the country a lasting part of their professional lives? Some are drawn to Vietnam out of a desire to make a small contribution to the country's development; some see an opportunity to make money; still others are lured by the sense of adventure and the excitement of living and working in a society that is changing at warp speed. Some veterans of what Vietnamese refer to as the "American War" come to find a measure of inner peace and an opportunity to create and renew rather than destroy. For some, working in Vietnam is a form of penance or partial repayment of an old debt.

For many Westerners, especially Americans, Vietnam is frozen in time, as the country was perceived during the war. The fact that Vietnam is at peace—and that it has been one country since 1975—comes as a surprise to many U.S. Americans and people of other nationalities, even some who live in Southeast Asia. Neil Jamieson points out in *Understanding Vietnam* that U.S. Americans have learned very little about Vietnam or the Vietnamese: books and movies about the war center mostly on the experience of being a U.S. American in Vietnam and shed little light on Vietnamese realities or perceptions. U.S. Americans, in Jamieson's view, "remain far too ready to assume that other people are, or want to be, or should be, like us" (1995, Preface).

Assuming that others are, want to be, or should be like us is, of course, a textbook version of cultural conditioning: "how people come by their behavior and especially why it is we are so intent on attributing our own behavioral norms to complete strangers from the other side of the planet" (Storti 1994). Milton J. Bennett refers to this as a minimization of cultural difference in which "differences are defined as relatively unimportant compared to the far more powerful dictates of cultural similarity" (1993, 41). It is a common mistake of those who remain within the confines of their own culture, blissfully ignorant of the world around them, with a tendency to rush to judgment and to view other societies as mirror images of themselves—to see more commonalities than actually exist.

Others have reduced Vietnam to a series of enduring stereotypes, a charge that Robert Templer, one-time journalist for Agence France-Presse and author of *Shadows and Wind: A View of Modern Vietnam,* first published in 1972, levels against Frances FitzGerald, the Pulitzer Prize–winning author of *Fire in the Lake.* By viewing the two nationalities as "reversed mirror images," Templer claims, FitzGerald absolves herself of the responsibility to learn more about the Vietnamese. U.S. Americans are creative, optimistic, and competitive, in this view, while Vietnamese "remain trapped in fixed intellectual and physical landscapes, completely beholden to the ageless and unbending forces of Confucianism, colonialism and village life" (1999, 17).

Regrettably, there are very few English-language works about Vietnamese culture and society. *Vietnam Today,* as a practical cultural guide, is intended to fill that gap and to help both those who travel to Vietnam as tourists and those who remain as long-term residents to negotiate their way through a labyrinth of customs and manners that are often alien to Westerners. It does not assume any prior knowledge of Vietnam and can be used by businesspeople, government officials, employees of international nongovernmental organizations (NGOs), and study-abroad participants; by professors of American Studies, Asian Studies, International Business, and other programs who are interested in integrating introductory material about Vietnam into their courses; by high school teachers of global studies and related courses; and by tourists, volunteers, and, in fact, all people who have an interest in learning more about contemporary Vietnamese culture—whether or not they have plans to travel to Vietnam in the near future.

In a class I teach to undergraduates, one of the themes, also relevant to *Vietnam Today,* is encapsulated in a sentiment I found spray-painted on a wall in Vienna, Austria, in the early 1980s: *Only those who move feel their chains.* Culture places constraints on our ways of thinking, doing, and interacting. Becoming interculturally competent is all about stretching our intellectual, emotional, and psychological horizons to the limit—and then some. To move and feel one's chains begins with that first step down the path of awareness and knowledge. To work (and play) with people from another culture, knowledge of that culture is not only highly advantageous but essential.

It is in this spirit that *Vietnam Today* is written—with an eye toward developing intercultural competence that is not merely the product of information and knowledge gleaned from a book but, rather, a skill that must be practiced, honed, and polished. In a 2003 Rand Corporation survey on "What Makes a Successful Career Professional in an International Organization," part of a larger study of multinational companies and international NGOs, "foreign-language fluency" ranked dead last (nineteenth), while "cross-cultural competence"—defined as "the ability to work well in different cultures and with people of different origins"—placed a very respectable fifth. Related items such as "interpersonal and relationship skills" and "ambiguity tolerance and adaptivity" ranked even higher—second and third, respectively.

In the course of our research for *Vietnam Today,* we interviewed and surveyed Vietnamese who have extensive experience with foreigners, particularly since the early 1990s. We did the same with expatriates from the U.S., England, France, and Australia, as well as with overseas Vietnamese, all of whom have worked or are still working in Vietnam. Some of the expatriates arrived just before the U.S. lifted its trade embargo in 1994; others have been there for only a few years. Together, they represent the trinity of private, public, and nongovernmental organization (NGO) sectors.

Because this is a book for Westerners, we have necessarily painted the comparisons between Vietnam and "the West" in broad strokes. There are simply too many differences between countries that fall under this latter rubric to merit a point-by-point comparison. In some cases, I will point out differences between specific Western cultures (French, Danish, U.S.) and Vietnamese culture. But for the most part *Vietnam Today* emphasizes the general differences between Vietnam as a Southeast Asian, relationship-based society—in which it is one's network of family, friends, colleagues, and others that is crucial to "getting things done"—on the one hand, and most Western, task-based countries—where there is a greater tendency to compartmentalize personal and professional relationships—on the other.

It should be noted that the focus of *Vietnam Today* is on Hanoi and HCM City, Vietnam's political and economic capitals, respectively. Although only 25 percent of Vietnam's population of over 80 million live in urban areas, these are the centers of power where most of the nation's business is conducted. If you travel to Vietnam, you should set aside time, however, to explore those off-the-beaten-path areas in the country-side where life has remained pretty much the same for generations. Not only will these excursions be enjoyable and educational, they also will help you see the larger picture and begin to decipher some of the con-nections between Vietnam's ancient past, dynamic present, and exciting future.

We want to add a note about the use of "Vietnam" versus "Viet Nam" in this book, as well as our approach to references to gender, overseas Vietnamese, and "America" and "Americans."

- **Vietnam:** We have chosen to use "Vietnam," rather than "Viet Nam," except in quoted text, titles, names of organizations, and specific historical references. "Vietnam" is the version that is most familiar to Westerners, and its use is in keeping with the central theme of this book. Similarly, we will use the English translation for names of cities—for example, "Hanoi" rather than "Ha Noi."
- **Pronouns:** For the sake of fairness, we use female and male pro-nouns interchangeably.
- **Overseas Vietnamese (*Viet kieu*):** We use this term to refer to those Vietnamese who have emigrated and are now part of the Viet-namese diaspora in Australia, Canada, France, Germany, the United States, and other countries.
- **U.S. Americans:** We use this term, which is more accurate than "Amer-icans," to refer to those from the United States, and, except where noted, we avoid the use of "America" to refer to the United States.

- **U.S.–Vietnam comparisons:** Although we have written *Vietnam Today* with Westerners in mind, occasional U.S.–Vietnam comparisons and contrasts inevitably surface. They reflect the unique relationship between the two countries, my intensely personal connection to the country from my vantage point as a U.S. citizen, and Diep's perspective as a Vietnamese who studied in the U.S.
- **Hanoi:** You may also detect a slight Hanoi slant. This reflects the fact that Diep is from Hanoi and I have conducted most of my "business" in the nation's capital, although I have traveled in the countryside and to central and southern Vietnam. You may assume that everything we present in *Vietnam Today* is generalizable, except where noted.

Vietnam Today is organized in a way that enables you to acquire some general information about Vietnam's political, social, and economic development, including the link between the country's turbulent yet inspirational history and the mind-set of the Vietnamese today, before proceeding to a discussion of specific cultural values, customs, and manners, and to Vietnamese impressions of Westerners.

Chapter 1, "Nation at a Crossroads," is a brief guided tour of Vietnam today, with some anecdotes illustrating just how much Vietnamese society has changed since the 1980s, how the ancient coexists with the modern, and how Marxism-Leninism and Ho Chi Minh Thought overlie a uniquely Vietnamese form of capitalism.

Chapter 2, "Country Overview," presents a wide-ranging overview of Vietnam, touching on geography, demographics, economic and political systems, religions, business environment, foreign investment and trade, tourism, overseas Vietnamese, and business centers.

Chapter 3, "A Brief History," describes Vietnam's two-thousand-year history of foreign invasion, occupation, and war and the far-reaching influence of that history on Vietnamese character, values, and aspirations. It draws on the work of several Vietnam experts and on the personal experiences of others who have spent extended periods of time living and working in Vietnam.

Chapter 4, "Vietnam at Peace," focuses on some of the defining issues and trends of the postwar era and their impact on the Vietnam of today, all of which are interrelated on some level. These include the economic reforms of 1986, corruption and bureaucracy, education and training, regional differences, and male–female relationships in the home, the larger society, and the workplace.

Chapter 5, "Core Cultural Dimensions," takes a more in-depth look at those characteristics that most distinguish Vietnam from the West, such as the importance of the group over the individual, relationship building as a prelude to doing business, and consensus building as the pillar of decision making. We will also look at how some core Vietnamese values influence verbal and nonverbal communication. Both this and the following chapter feature cross-cultural dialogues that illustrate important cultural points.

Chapter 6, "Working with the Vietnamese," offers practical tips, including dos and don'ts for initiating a relationship, preparing for and conducting business meetings, and socializing. This chapter also includes information about negotiating strategies and decision-making styles, and about how to maintain a long-term relationship successfully.

Chapter 7, "How the Vietnamese See Westerners," presents impressions and reflections—positive, negative, and constructively critical—from Vietnamese who have worked with foreigners for many years. It is a small-scale attempt to look into the cultural mirror and raise the level of understanding between peoples who know far too little about each other. It contains valuable advice that reinforces and affirms much of what appears elsewhere in *Vietnam Today,* especially in Chapters 5 and 6.

Chapter 8, "Epilogue," concludes with a brief look at Vietnam in the new century, including some predictions about the shape and form of a Vietnamese society undergoing rapid change and opening up to the world, and speculation about some of the possible implications of these changes for cross-cultural interaction.

To visit Vietnam now—whether as a student interested in its language and culture, a veteran who wishes to experience the country at peace, a businessperson interested in selling or buying, a volunteer whose

objective is to contribute in some modest way to the country's development, or simply a tourist who wishes to enjoy the people and the natural
scenic beauty of the country—is to become a witness to history in the
making and, for U.S. Americans and others, to play a role in the reconciliation of former enemies. As many expatriates freely admit—an admission
that is something of a secret outside of their closed community—Vietnam can be a great place to live and work.

Let me conclude this section with two impressions from foreigners
who ended up working in Vietnam for many years.

> I loved the people, the food, the smiles on the faces of children,
> the scenery, the pace of life. Like many foreigners, I was frustrated
> by the infrastructure: electrical blackouts, floods, traffic, and
> maniac drivers.

> I love the friendliness and kindness of the people. I love the food,
> the beauty of the landscapes and the architecture, and the high
> energy level of the streets in small villages and large cities alike.
> Dislikes? Having to return home. . . .

Nation at a Crossroads

Viet Nam is now at a crossroads and must decide whether short-term economic growth should take precedence over the long-term struggle to broaden the horizons of human freedom.

—WILLIAM DUIKER

The Vietnam of today is full of promise and potential, pulsating with energy and steeped in dreams. At the same time, Vietnam has entered the twenty-first century faced with a range of pressing political, social, and economic problems—some the result of bad policies, mismanagement, and ideological rigidity, others the legacy of colonialism, war, and subsequent attempts to punish the country for political reasons. At the same time, those who come with a knowledge of Vietnamese culture and the ability to connect and adapt—along with an abundance of energy, patience, perseverance, flexibility, humor, and commitment—will be well positioned to bridge the cultural chasm that separates Vietnamese culture from that of the West.

If you arrive in Hanoi in the summer, or in Ho Chi Minh (HCM) City (formerly Saigon) at any time of year, expect to be enveloped by a thick blanket of heat and humidity the second you step out of the air-conditioned airport. Also expect to have your senses assaulted by the kaleidoscopic smells, both tantalizing and nauseating, and sounds, both wondrous and earsplitting, of a developing tropical country. Your first walk across a street in either city will be a test of your ability to keep your wits about you, to be aware of everyone and everything around you, and to reach the other side safely by walking in measured steps and at a steady pace, allowing—*trusting*—drivers to glide around you, in effect putting your health, and possibly your life, in their hands. As one first-time visitor put it, "to cross the street requires nerves of steel, a Buddha's inner calm, or, failing that, a stiff drink" (McLane 2004). Welcome to Vietnam!

Walking around, you soon discover that very few aspects of the physical environment are uniform and predictable, as in most Western countries. Beware of holes, wires not adjusted to the height of the average Westerner, unexpected steps, and other idiosyncrasies that reflect uneven development and progress on both literal and figurative levels. For example, though Hanoi now has stoplights, human beings still lower the gate before an approaching train rumbles by.

Foreigners who visit Vietnam for the first time often succumb to a myopic view of the country, making snap judgments based on limited experience. Resist the temptation to jump to conclusions based on minimal information or to attempt to make Vietnam conform to your preconceived, culturally shaped perceptions of what is real, what is normal. Consider traffic, for example. Traffic in Vietnam's cities may appear at a glance to be chaotic and disorganized, but it can also be seen as an organic whole in which every participant is in fact working in tandem with everyone else—seemingly competitive, but cooperative as well. As if following some societal law of physics, spaces are filled almost as quickly as they open up. As you cross a street, you need to remain alert, sensitive to everything going on around you. And this applies also to your interactions with Vietnamese: you must learn to read between the lines, to become able to hear the true meaning behind their words, their silence, and their body language.

There are many more examples of how Westerners in Vietnam may leap too quickly to conclusions. Here are just a few:

- You may conclude that Vietnam's cities are filthy because you see so many bags of trash lying in the gutters. In fact, they are waiting to be picked up by the legion of efficient, blue-shirted sanitation workers, wearing conical hats, who load them onto waiting garbage trucks.
- You may be surprised to see men holding hands in a country in which homosexuality is taboo. In fact, holding hands or walking arm in arm is acceptable among friends of the same sex, while generally frowned upon for members of the opposite sex. (Like so many other things in Vietnamese culture, this, too, is changing.)
- You may notice that some men have abnormally long fingernails by Western standards. No, they are not being effeminate; they are just making it clear that they are not manual laborers.
- Young women driving motorbikes may appear to be making a fashion statement by wearing gloves and covering their arms. In fact, they are trying to avoid getting a suntan in a society that values light over dark skin, because the latter is equated with working in the fields from dawn to dusk.

We fall into the trap of using our own culture as a frame of reference, and lack an appreciation for and understanding of the radical transformation that Vietnam has undergone since the early 1990s. Developments that many visitors take for granted—the telecommunications system, the availability and quality of consumer goods, and the depth and breadth of the hospitality industry, including Vietnamese and foreign restaurants, cafés, nightclubs, and karaoke—were unimaginable just a few years ago. Restaurants featuring foreign cuisine, which used to cater to a largely foreign clientele, are now frequented by young urban Vietnamese who can easily afford the comparatively higher prices.

Twenty years ago, making telephone calls across town could be problematic; now Vietnamese with Internet access are chatting with people around the world, and motorbike drivers can be seen talking on cell phones or sending text messages while cruising along at thirty-five miles

an hour. Even the ways young people express affection toward one another have changed in the past ten years: whereas traditionally it was
acceptable to hold hands only with a friend of the same sex, today it is
common to see young men and women walking down the street hand in
hand. And marriages between Vietnamese and foreigners, though still
rare, are increasing in number and in degree of social acceptance.

The Hanoi and HCM City of 2004 bear little resemblance to their
former selves in the immediate postwar period. As recently as the early
1990s, both cities were described as sleepy towns. Those were the days
when Vietnam was just beginning to reform its economy and open up to
the rest of world. It was before the presence of disposable income that
enables people to purchase motorbikes, cars, cell phones, and fashionable
clothes, or to go out for a night on the town; before the appearance of foreigners from anywhere other than the Soviet Union and the countries of
Eastern Europe; before the advent of information technology that would
link Vietnam with the global community.

Hoan Kiem Lake, one of the jewels of Hanoi and its main tourist area,
is now brimming with activity—foreigners and Vietnamese making their
rounds, young people whispering sweet nothings into each other's ears
after sunset, the steady drone of traffic, restaurants and shops in every
direction, people sitting in a café overlooking the city sipping lime juice
and eating coconut ice cream. In the mid-1980s, it was a quieter, darker,
almost serene place, with only the whir of bicycle tires, the muffled sounds
of voices, and the occasional Russian. The gardens were not as well main-
tained in those days, and few shops beckoned customers.

An expat who spent many years in Vietnam remembers the Hanoi of
1992—daily blackouts, very few paved roads, dirty streets. She recalls how
she was unable to ask many questions outside of family or general cultural information, and also how she was asked in shops and on the street
if she was Russian (at a time when most of the foreigners in Vietnam were
in fact Russian).

Another Westerner, who arrived in 1994 to begin establishing his company's presence in Vietnam, trained everyone on his fledging staff except
the driver ("the only one who knew his job"). His most important decision

at the time? Hiring his first local employee, who is still with the firm—a decision he says he made on the basis of "gut instinct." Nowadays, according to this employer, hiring is much easier in terms of both job seekers' qualifications and the ability to talk to other people about job applicants.

Just ten years ago, shortly after the trade embargo was lifted, Coca-Cola—much to the dismay and anger of the Vietnamese—was erecting giant billboards across the street from the historic opera house in Hanoi in a race to capture the nascent cola market. Today, sophisticated Western-style advertising in Vietnamese and English graces the city's skyline in the form of billboards and signs, and TV commercials cater to a rapidly growing urban middle class. The effect of seeing this sort of advertising side by side with hand-painted posters and billboards exhorting people to have only two children, to beware of the dangers of HIV/AIDS, and to vote in an upcoming election can be a bit surreal.

Although Vietnam is still a poor country plagued by many of the problems that characterize the developing world, including corruption, child malnutrition, environmental degradation, unemployment, and underemployment—and, unlike many other developing countries, has had to cope with the additional legacy of being at war for two generations—it has made stunning progress on the home front and in the steps it has taken to become a full-fledged member of the international community. And—also unlike many other developing countries—Vietnam is stable and safe, with a government that is generally committed to improving the lives of its citizens.

Although the market reforms of the late 1980s have contributed to Vietnam's recovery and to a stratospheric economic growth rate, they have also led to a widening gap between rich and poor and to a rural–urban migration, as in China, that the nation's cities simply cannot absorb. In the prologue to *Hanoi: City of the Rising Dragon,* the authors have this to say about the "renovation" and its prospects for success:

> . . . this renovation, if it is genuine and characterized by openness
> to a market economy, still has a long way to go. The ideologues
> have not had their last word yet, and the countless survivors of

Vietnam's many battles may well question the ambiguity of liberation, of national unification, of a socialist system that offers no prospects for the popular majority, and of economic development that only aggravates inequality. But it could not be otherwise in a system that encourages opportunity businesspeople and foreign investment but does not resolve problems like overpopulation, dilapidated housing, poor sanitation, or schools that are deserted because of high tuition and low teacher salaries. (Boudarel and Nguyen 2002, 6)

There are other, less tangible changes that may reflect a shift in values, especially among the younger generation, from a collectivist to a more individualist orientation, the result of a market economy that emphasizes competition, image, and consumerism. Nevertheless, although money has increased in figurative value, a sense of community and the family remain important to Vietnamese of all ages and backgrounds.

Gone are the old days when people pretended to be poor so that it would not appear that they were becoming capitalistic, a fear that resulted from years of centralized economic planning in the North. That was a time when a family would sell its food vouchers on the free (read "black") market in order to buy good meat, say, or fish, and prepare a feast for the entire family. Then, so as not to draw attention to themselves in the neighborhood, they would stagger the visits of aunts, uncles, and grandparents throughout the day. Similarly, in another example of savoring a rare treat in secrecy, one family adopted the practice of cutting a chicken with scissors rather than a knife to ensure that the process was a quiet and inconspicuous one. Only during Tet (the Lunar New Year) and for meals honoring ancestors would they use a knife to cut up the chicken.

Poverty is the great equalizer, and there was a time when the Vietnamese were unified and in solidarity in terms of what they had—and, during wartime, in relation to the common enemy against which they fought. Personal initiative and risk taking in pursuit of material gain were not valued commodities under the old system. The emphasis, for both historical and political reasons, was on "safety in numbers" and working together for the common good, which frequently involved prolonged resistance against a foreign invader and physical survival.

It was a view that prevailed until quite recently. I remember cruising around Hanoi in the mid-1990s with an acquaintance in his shiny new Mercedes while he spoke of the government's ambivalent view of the private sector and of the gnawing feeling that he could become a victim of his own success. Aside from his luxury German car, one of the few in Hanoi at that time and his only ostentatious display of wealth, his lifestyle did not reflect his status as a multimillionaire. Now, less than ten years later, the official view of the private sector is supportive, and the number of luxury cars driven by Vietnamese has skyrocketed, a barometer of increasing urban wealth.

For better and for worse, the consumer economy has arrived with a vengeance in Vietnam, particularly in the cities. In the Vietnam of 2004, especially among the members of the urban elite, the trend is to show off one's financial well-being, whether by wearing name-brand clothes (even if they are domestically produced rip-offs) and expensive jewelry, or by driving a high-end motorbike or car. Competition is making inroads in a collectivist society, and inequality of income and wealth is on the rise. To use the traffic analogy again, one's mode of transportation is a probable indicator of social class—from car to motorbike to bicycle to that behemoth of the road, the humble bus.

Of course, these changes range from the superficial to the substantive, encompassing the physical, economic, and legal infrastructure of the country. They are also fundamental and irreversible. There are few places in the world where so much has changed in so short a time. The atmosphere in Vietnam, especially in the cities, is electric, the energy of the people palpable. The country continues to forge ahead and may well achieve its goal of institutionalizing a "market economy with socialist orientation," or "red capitalism," guided by an authoritarian, centralized government with a ruling elite.

CHAPTER TWO

Country Overview

*Vietnam could become the Taiwan of Southeast Asia in the
next twenty years.*

—European expatriate

This chapter presents a general overview of Vietnam, including geography, demographics, the economic and political systems, the business environment, and foreign investment. The intent here is to provide some basic background information before going on to a more detailed discussion of other aspects of Vietnamese culture and society.

Geography

Vietnam, which has been described as a shoulder pole with a rice basket at each end, stretches in an S-shape from China in the north to the Gulf of Thailand in the south. In the center, near Hue, only 50 kilometers (about 30 miles) separate the South China Sea (known as the East Sea in Vietnam) from Laos. Situated in the center of Southeast Asia, closer to the Tropic of Cancer than to the Equator, Vietnam offers everything from tropical coastal lowlands to temperate zones above 2,000 meters (about 6,500 feet) in elevation. To put these facts and figures in perspective, consider that most of this geographic diversity is condensed into an area than can be covered in a two-hour flight from Hanoi in the North to HCM City in the South.

Vietnam is a lush, verdant country defined by the color green and by the element of water. Rice paddies in low-lying areas stretch as far as the eye can see; cash crops such as coffee and rubber thrive in the Central Highlands, rice, bananas, sugarcane, and coconuts in the Mekong Delta region. There are also rolling hills covered with thick jungle and jagged mountains rising more than 3,000 meters (nearly 10,000 feet) into the sky, the jutting limestone rock formations in the aqua blue waters of the East Sea and over 3,200 kilometers (about 2,000 miles) of coastline with pristine white sand beaches. Seventy-five percent of the country consists of mountains and hills, including spectacular mountain ranges in the northern and central regions, running along the border with Laos and Cambodia.

Vietnam has an amazingly varied climate, ranging from very hot in the South to bitterly cold and (on rare occasions) even snowy in the mountains near the Chinese border. Visitors to the North are often surprised by the region's distinct seasons: an oppressively hot, humid summer followed by a pleasant and, as the locals say, "romantic" autumn with the scent of seasonal flowers in the air, then a cool to cold winter punctuated by damp, penetrating drizzles, and finally a spring that begins warming up shortly after Tet, the Vietnamese Lunar New Year. During a May trip to Hanoi, there were days when it was actually cooler than in my home state of New York, an example of how temperatures can fluctuate before summer arrives. In July, the average temperature in Hanoi is a steamy 28.6°C (83.5°F), in Hue 28.9°C (84°F), and in HCM City 27.6°C (82°F). Humidity can reach 90 percent in the rainy season, from May to October. In the South, the year-round midday heat is mitigated by sudden showers, which have a welcome moderating effect, and by an occasional cool tropical breeze.

Most of the population is found in the two main cultivated areas, the Red River Delta in the North and the Mekong Delta in the South. Central and northern Vietnam are at greatest risk for seasonal flooding precipitated by the heavy rains and typhoons that develop between July and

November. Flooding of the Mekong River is less severe than along the Red River, where, when flood control measures (a system of dikes and levees) fail, the results can be catastrophic. The change in seasons and its impact on the environment and the people is obvious when seen from the air— villages like islands, with rivers and their tributaries spreading out over the countryside in all directions. It is one of the forces of nature that the Vietnamese have lived with and attempted to control for millennia.

People

The first and lasting impressions of the Vietnamese people are of their warmth, adaptability, work ethic, tenacity, energy, humor, optimism, and love of country. The Vietnamese, despite what they and their country have suffered at the hands of the U.S., France, Japan, and China, among other foreign powers, find inspiration in the past and look to the future with great optimism and hope. If you are bold enough to begin learning the language, which will permit you a fuller appreciation and understanding of the people and their culture, you will even discover that people are appreciative, patient, and happy to correct your mistakes not with admonitions and disdain but with gentleness and respect.

Ethnicity

Although Vietnam's population includes fifty-four ethnic groups, each with its own language, it is nonetheless relatively homogeneous. About 90 percent of the population consists of ethnic Vietnamese, most of whom live in lowland areas in the North (Red River Delta) and South (Mekong Delta). Another fifty-two ethnic groups account for 7 percent of the population, living mostly in the central and northern mountainous areas of the country. Ethnic Chinese, the largest minority group, make up the remaining 3 percent. Most live in southern Vietnam, particularly in the Cholon district of HCM City.

The government's mistrust and wrath with respect to things Chinese has made the ethnic Chinese Vietnamese perennial targets of discrimination and victims of periodic expulsions. The majority of the so-called boat people who fled Vietnam after the war in several waves are of Chinese ancestry. In 1978, the government implemented a series of anticapitalist measures that included the confiscation of private property and businesses, many of which belonged to ethnic Chinese. It is estimated that around 450,000 ethnic Chinese left Vietnam from 1978 to 1989, either by boat or over the border into China. As elsewhere in Asia, they are best known for their business acumen and well-organized regional and international networks.

Population

By 2003, Vietnam's population had reached 81 million, making it the fourteenth most populous country in the world. Although Vietnam has endured centuries of war, including most recently the First Indochina War against France and the Second Indochina War against the U.S., its population growth was quite high from 1960 to 1975, at slightly over 3 percent annually. At the end of the Vietnam War in 1975, a baby boom pushed Vietnam's population to unsustainable levels, and in 1976 the government issued a two-child-only directive. Now, after many years of this policy, Vietnam's population growth rate has stabilized and, in fact, declined to a rate of less than 2 percent annually. In response, the government has removed the limit on the number of children, a shift that will likely lead to an increase in the birth rate. This, in turn, may eventually have deleterious effects on the nation's education system and on a strained labor market that is currently unable to absorb the large number of new workers entering the work force each year.

For historical reasons, which will be discussed in Chapter 3, Vietnam's population is exceptionally young. Approximately half of the Vietnamese are under twenty-five.

Religion

Vietnam's religious diversity reflects the country's experience with foreign invaders and occupiers, as well as its status as a crossroads of trade in Southeast Asia. There are four major religions in Vietnam: Buddhism, Confucianism, Taoism, and Christianity. Most Vietnamese practice what is known as the "triple religion," a mixture of Buddhism, Taoism, and Confucianism.

Theravada Buddhism arrived in Vietnam via Indian trade routes through present-day Myanmar (formerly Burma) and Thailand. Mahayana Buddhism came later, during Chinese rule, and emerged as the official state religion after Vietnam regained its independence in the tenth century. Buddhism is based on these Four Noble Truths:

- Existence is suffering.
- Suffering is caused by desire.
- Suffering ends with the extinction of desire.
- To end suffering, follow the steps of the Eightfold Path: right understanding (or views), thought, speech, action, livelihood, effort, mindfulness, and concentration (or meditation).

Confucianism emphasizes social behavior, duty, and hierarchy more than religious practices. Its code of ethics demands loyalty of government to the emperor, obedience of children to parents, and submission of wives to husbands. It asserts that everyone has the same potential for achieving happiness, attained by improvement through education. Confucian ideals also promote ancestor worship, the ritual expression of filial piety.

The Temple of Literature (Van Mieu), built in the twelfth century in present-day Hanoi, is dedicated to Confucius. It is the site of the first university in Vietnam and for many centuries was the principal center of learning. Aside from being a major tourist attraction, the temple is still used as a place of worship, with many altars of burning incense and statues of the Buddha.

Christianity was introduced to Vietnam in the seventeenth century by missionaries from Spain, Portugal, and France. There are nearly six million Catholics, most of whom live in the south. A small number of Vietnamese are Muslims, mainly from the Chan ethnic minority group living in central Vietnam.

Although Vietnam's constitution guarantees religious freedom, the government does not tolerate attempts on the part of religious groups or organizations to oppose it. A new State Ordinance on Beliefs and Religions outlines cases in which belief and religious activities will be temporarily suspended. As one example, mentioned by the deputy head of the Government Committee for Religious Affairs in a recent interview, such a suspension would occur if "someone takes advantage of their religious freedom to threaten national security and the people's solidarity" (*http://vietnamnews.vnagency.com.vn/2004-07/24/Comment.htm*).

Languages

The Vietnamese language, which, like Chinese and Thai, is tonal (that is, one word may have several different meanings depending on the speaker's tone), is the official language of Vietnam, spoken by a majority of the population. Regional accents are noticeable in the North, center, and South, but in most cases such differences do not preclude mutual understanding. Thanks to Alexander de Rhodes, a seventeenth-century missionary who mastered and transcribed the language into the Latin alphabet, Vietnamese—a musical language that de Rhodes likened to the chattering of birds—is much easier to read than to speak and understand.

Most of the ethnic minorities who live in the mountainous regions, while preserving their own languages, study and speak Vietnamese. There are exceptions, however, and these are determined by economic priorities. For those who live in areas that attract large numbers of tourists, such as Sapa, a charming town near the Chinese border that is a former French colonial outpost, many members of ethnic minorities who make their living selling arts-and-crafts items to foreigners may speak better English than Vietnamese.

Since the collapse of the Soviet Union, which coincided with Vietnam's market reforms and gradual integration into the global economy, Russian has long since been replaced by English as the country's second language, followed by French, Chinese, and Japanese. Many older people speak French, and quite a few middle-aged Vietnamese who studied in Russia and Eastern Europe speak the languages of those countries. Khmer (Cambodian) and various tribal languages have recently been introduced in some colleges and universities, and some specialized graduate programs are even offered in English.

Although language proficiency is the key to becoming truly bicultural—and Vietnamese respect people who make the attempt to learn their admittedly difficult language—it is only the select few who are able to make the long-term commitment necessary to attain functional proficiency in Vietnamese. Those who do so usually have studied the language formally for several years before coming to Vietnam, have spent at least a year in-country enrolled in a high-quality language class—and also are likely to be gifted language learners. Most expatriates in Vietnam (that is, in Hanoi and HCM City) speak Vietnamese poorly or not at all. A Vietnamese manager who has worked with foreigners for many years asserted that although Vietnamese respect people who try to learn their language, it is more important that foreigners be culturally aware, act in culturally appropriate ways, and be able to develop and maintain relationships.

Literacy

Vietnam has a literacy rate of 94 percent, an extraordinary figure for a developing country with a high level of poverty. This can be explained in part by the Confucian respect for and value on education, as well as by successes in universalizing primary education. The Vietnamese are insatiable readers; within a system that restricts freedom of the press, they have a wide array of newspapers, magazines, and books from which to choose. (In 2002, nearly seven million issues of newspapers were published in Vietnam, eight for every man, woman, and child.) The country's high literacy rate—combined with the low cost of labor and the renowned Vietnamese work ethic—is another selling point in the government's attempt to attract more foreign investment.

Politics and Administration

While seemingly rigid to the outside observer and, like most political systems, riddled with inconsistencies and canyon-like gaps between rhetoric and reality, Vietnam has succeeded in maintaining stability and peace for all of its citizens and a rising tide of prosperity for growing segments of its population, especially in urban areas. Contrary to the widely held view of one-party states where everyone walks in lockstep, blindly following a narrowly defined party line, there are many divergent views and disagreements in Vietnam about such macro-level issues as the overall direction in which the country should be heading as well as micro-level issues, like whether karaoke is a "social evil" or the right of every Vietnamese citizen. (Of course, there is also the split between public and private criticism, which is not unique to Vietnam.) What is undeniable is that party and state have chosen to bend rather than break at recent watershed moments, such as the shift from centralized planning to a free-market economy.

Communist Party of Vietnam

Although the 1992 Constitution outlined a reorganization of the government and increased freedom, notably economic freedom, Vietnam remains a one-party state controlled by the Communist Party of Vietnam (CPV), reaffirmed by the Constitution as the leading force of state and society. The CPV leads the National Assembly and people's councils and is responsible for charting the direction of development, mapping out strategies, and formulating policies for the country.

The Party exercises leadership through its organizational structure in state bodies and political and social mass organizations, as well as through Party committees and their members. The direction of the Party and the government is set at the Party Congress, which meets every five years. A 150-member Central Committee elected by the Party Congress usually meets at least twice a year. The Party has about two million members, amounting to less than 2.5 percent of the population; it is interesting to note that Vietnam's Catholic population (about six million) far exceeds the number of Party members.

Much of the CPV's claim to legitimacy rests on the past—its victory over the French and the U.S. and its role in unifying the country. In some respects, the Party functions as a government unto itself, funded by a combination of membership dues, business deals, and the state treasury. In Vietnam as in China, *the overriding goal is to grow the economy while maintaining control.* The focus has long since shifted from the Party's past glories and achievements to current and future challenges, both domestic and foreign. The CPV will ultimately be judged on the extent to which it can bring economic prosperity to more segments of the population and grapple with problems that are the result of Vietnam's economic reforms.

National Assembly

As Vietnam's highest representative legislative body, the National Assembly is the highest organ of state power. It drafts legislation and supervises compliance with the laws it passes. The National Assembly has a broad mandate to oversee all government functions, and it decides important issues related to national policy and people's livelihoods, mainly in the areas of planning and budget. About 80 percent of the deputies to the National Assembly are Party members. The assembly meets twice a year for seven to ten weeks at a time; elections are held every five years.

The Government

The Party is the leader, but the state is in charge of managing the country's development. The government is the executive body, and the president, as head of state, is responsible for internal management and external relations. The president also serves as the nominal commander of the armed forces and as chairman of the Council on National Defense and Security. The prime minister is head of the government, which consists of four deputy prime ministers and the heads of thirty-one ministries and commissions, all confirmed by the National Assembly. Both president and prime minister are elected and serve at the pleasure of the National Assembly.

People's Organizations

People's organizations are a structure that has existed in Vietnam for more than seventy years, creating a route by which the Party's policies reach the people and, in turn, the people's concerns reach the Party. Sometimes collectively called the Homeland Front, these organizations include, among others, the Women's Union, the Farmers' Union, trade unions, professional groups, religious organizations, and the Red Cross. As just one example of how these organizations operate, it is noteworthy that one of the driving forces behind the renovation of the 1980s, discussed in the next section, was the action of several localities that privatized their rice paddies, reaped increased yields, and then used their results to lobby for change.

Economy

In the early 1980s, Vietnam began its transformation into a multisector, market-based economy. It was a time when Vietnam's economy, after several decades of following a Soviet-style economic model based on centralized planning, was suffering from massive economic inefficiency. Human, fixed, and institutional capital were misallocated and poorly utilized. The situation was so dire that it could have led to a collapse of the economy if the government had not implemented drastic reforms. After 1986, when renovation began in earnest, Vietnam's economy took off with such impressive growth that many international analysts and economists predicted that the country would become one of Asia's next economic tigers. This rapid improvement in Vietnam's economic performance resulted in sweeping social and economic changes. From 1989 to 1995, Vietnam enjoyed a rapid increase in the influx of foreign investment, with real GDP growth greater than 8 percent in 1992 and 9.5 percent in 1995, contributing to a reduction in the poverty rate and an improvement in living standards.

By the onset of the Asian economic crisis in July 1997, however, the rate of growth had already begun to decelerate. Many foreign investment projects were canceled, and a decrease in exports resulted in a decline in economic growth. In 1999, Vietnam's GDP was only 4.8 percent, just half of the 1995 rate of 9.5 percent, contributing to a rise in unemployment and poverty. Since 2000, an economic recovery has been underway. Despite weakening exports and agricultural output, Vietnam's economy remained healthy, with stable prices and solid indicators of public finance and external debt in 2001.

In 2002, Vietnam's economy performed well, with GDP growth of 7 percent, marking another milestone in its economic development. This considerable achievement was boosted by a substantial increase in exports to the U.S.—crude oil, footwear, coffee, and textiles, among others—thanks to the U.S.–Vietnam Bilateral Trade Agreement, which came into effect in December 2001. Vietnam's brisk economic growth continued during the first half of 2003 despite the impact of the SARS (severe acute respiratory syndrome) epidemic. Export earnings increased by nearly 17 percent, and GDP continued to grow at just over 7 percent.

Clearly, eighteen years of economic reforms have opened Vietnam to the outside world and spurred high economic growth. They ended decades of isolation and jump-started an array of economic and social reforms. Vietnam is now committed to global economic integration through its participation in global and regional trade organizations such as Asia-Pacific Economic Cooperation (APEC), the Association of Southeast Asian Nations (ASEAN) Free Trade Area, and World Trade Organization (WTO) accession negotiations, with a target entry date of 2005.

Business Environment

The Vietnamese government has made great strides in creating a more efficient and open business environment by improving its legal framework and deregulating access to the market. The Enterprise Law of 2000 laid the groundwork for a healthy business environment by easing obstacles to entry, removing licensing requirements for more than half of the subsectors, lowering registration costs, and dramatically shortening the approval process for start-ups. And the response from Vietnam's fledgling private sector has been encouraging—36,000 newly registered small and medium-sized businesses now employ more than 500,000 workers, 1.5 percent of the total workforce.

An amendment to the existing Law on Foreign Direct Investment has provided better treatment for foreign and jointly owned enterprises, with more efficient procedures for foreign direct investment. Key provisions of the amendment, aimed at simplifying the registration of foreign-invested businesses, allow greater access to foreign exchange, clarify government guarantees on certain types of infrastructure projects, and encourage investment by overseas Vietnamese. Further, a Competition and Anti-Monopoly Law, drafted by the government to encourage fair competition and to protect businesses from unfair competition practices and competition restraints, is expected to make Vietnam's business environment more stable, predictable, and attractive.

Legal System

The Vietnamese legal system is based on communist legal theory and the French civil law system. The system encompasses a constitution and various codes, laws, ordinances, decrees, decisions, circulars, directives, and official letters—all of which have the force of law, although only a law passed by the National Assembly is referred to as such. Ordinances issued by the Standing Committee of the National Assembly regulate areas in which a law has not yet been promulgated. On matters that the National Assembly entrusts to the government, the latter issues decrees, decisions, or directives to implement the relevant laws or ordinances. Circulars, decisions, and regulations are normally issued by individual ministers and other heads of state agencies with respect to areas within their sphere of responsibility and have the force of subordinate legislation.

Since the policy of economic reform shifted the country to a socialist market-driven economy, Vietnam has amended its existing laws as well as enacting new laws. A multisector economic system and individual ownership were recognized through the amendment to the 1989 constitution's new revised Civil Code. In addition, the National Assembly has passed many other laws and ordinances governing the functioning of a market economy.

Foreign Investment in Vietnam

Vietnam only began to open up to foreign investment in 1987. The first Foreign Investment Law was passed in December 1988, and numerous regulations to encourage investment were introduced and amended over the years. From the late 1980s to the mid-1990s, there was a large increase in investment, followed by a drastic decline with the Asian crisis of 1997. Today, the investment climate is improving slowly, and the government has once more amended the investment law to encourage foreign companies to invest.

Most foreign direct investment (FDI) in Vietnam is concentrated in capital-intensive projects and industries, such as automobile, motorbike, cement, and steel production, which currently are protected. As such protection comes to an end in 2006, this pattern of FDI will no longer work in Vietnam. Those seeking to invest in protected industries will face fierce competition and, as a result, will probably move their production to other countries where such protections still exist.

Foreign Trade

Since Vietnam's trade was liberalized in 1986, its export earnings have increased rapidly, from less than $1 billion in 1987 to more than $15 billion in 2001. In 2002, export revenues were at $16.5 billion, and exports for 2003 were forecast around $20 billion. The lifting of the trade embargo and the Bilateral Trade Agreement with the United States are two obvious reasons for this impressive growth. Vietnam is rich in natural resources and agricultural goods; its major export earners are crude oil, seafood, rice, and coffee. An abundance of relatively low cost and skilled labor has fueled Vietnam's exports in such labor-intensive industries as textiles, garments, and footwear.

Major export destinations include the U.S., Japan, the European Union countries (especially Germany, the U.K., and France), China, Singapore, Taiwan, and Australia. Following the signing of the U.S.–Vietnam Bilateral Trade Agreement, export to this market increased exponentially, from virtually zero in early 1990 to well over $2 billion in 2002 and nearly $3 billion in 2003, and the U.S. catapulted ahead of Japan to become the largest single-country market for Vietnamese exports.

Imports have grown steadily since the late 1980s as the result of an increasing demand for raw materials and capital equipment relating to manufactured exports. In 2002, import values exceeded $19 billion, resulting in a trade deficit of nearly $3 billion in U.S. dollars. Major imports include machinery (around 25 percent of total imports), raw materials, petroleum products, and various food products. The major sources of imports are Taiwan, Singapore, Japan, South Korea, China, and the United States.

Overseas Vietnamese

Vietnam also generates substantial foreign-exchange earnings from Vietnamese workers overseas and from foreign tourists. In addition to sending remittances amounting to an estimated $2 billion a year, many overseas Vietnamese have returned for the short or long term to start businesses. They bring with them not only capital but also their knowledge, experience, contacts, Vietnamese proficiency, and cultural familiarity.

Tourism

In 2002, Vietnam hosted 2.6 million tourists, about 250,000 of them U.S. Americans, including veterans returning for the first time; tourists from Japan ranked second. Although Vietnam attracts visitors from all over the world, particularly Australia, East Asia, and Europe, as well as the U.S., the government is especially interested in the large and potentially lucrative U.S. market. As Vu The Binh, director of Vietnam's Tourism Department, pointed out during an August 2003 visit to San Francisco for tourism and trade promotion, "We think that tourism is the best way to promote the establishment of friendly relations between the two countries." The choice of California—home to 500,000 of the United States' 1.2 million Vietnamese Americans—and of the Bay Area in particular was no coincidence: San Francisco entered into a sister-city relationship with HCM City in the late 1990s. There are plans for Vietnam Airlines, the national flag carrier, which has an office in San Francisco, to begin the first direct U.S.–Vietnam flights in the near future. Saigontourist, Vietnam's largest commercial tour operator, is identifying a location in downtown San Francisco for a Vietnam tourism and cultural center.

"There are five million American soldiers who were in Vietnam," Vu said on his San Francisco visit. "Then there are their children and grandchildren. That's a lot of people." This upbeat assessment and tendency to see the silver lining in the clouds reflect the dynamism and optimism of Vietnam's market economy and global orientation.

There are many obvious reasons why foreign tourists flock to Vietnam, including the country's breathtaking natural beauty, geographic and ethnic diversity, fascinating history, and low cost. An additional feature that enhances Vietnam's attractiveness is its safety, especially in the wake of the terrorist attacks in Bali, Indonesia. One Vietnamese travel company, founded in 1996, has benefited from both this perception and the reality it reflects: the company now boasts ten thousand clients who travel to exotic destinations in Vietnam, Cambodia, and elsewhere in Southeast Asia.

Vietnam's reputation as one of the safest and most politically stable countries in Southeast Asia has also worked in its favor on the economic front, as multinational companies weigh the risks of doing business in neighboring countries such as Malaysia, Indonesia, and the Philippines, which have been recent sources and targets of terrorism.

Business Centers

Hanoi, the capital of Vietnam with about three million people, is the site of government ministries, international NGOs, and embassies. For anyone who wishes to conduct business in Vietnam, all roads run through Hanoi. The city itself is a charming relic of the French colonial era, dotted with picturesque parks and lakes and replete with tree-lined boulevards and restored villas that are now offices or embassies, as well as plenty of newly constructed apartment and office buildings.

Like HCM City, Vietnam's economic capital, Hanoi is a densely populated environment with a prolonged "rush hour" during which virtually every square meter of road is occupied by a vehicle of some sort, mostly motorbikes, all trying to make their way to work, home, or wherever, as quickly as possible. As in other cities in Vietnam, much of life in Hanoi is lived on the streets—eating, drinking, exercising, socializing, earning a living. An expat with considerable experience in all three regions of Vietnam describes Hanoi as slower and more cumbersome in relationships but adds that the people are friendlier and the culture more distinctly Vietnamese.

In *Hanoi: City of the Rising Dragon,* the authors describe this symbol of Vietnam as follows:

> The ancient city was rich in history, legends, myths, thus assuring its role as guardian of the Vietnamese identity. Hanoi remained strong despite Viet Nam's tumultuous contradictions: between rupture and continuity, revolt and submission, freedom of speech and operational secrets, human rights and totalitarian power, the intrusion of Western modernity and the preservation of tradition, and finally socialism and a market economy. Its ambivalence, as much as its topography, justifies the name Hanoi, which means "amid the rivers." (Boudarel and Nguyen 2002, 1)

"Ha Noi," representing the Vietnamese pronunciation of two Chinese characters, "river" and "inside," is a city on the move and in an expansion mode, as evidenced by the cost of real estate in the outlying areas and the frenzy of construction in areas that not too long ago were rice paddies. As in other countries, wealth in Vietnam is acquired by several means— through knowing the right people, by building a successful business, or by owning real estate. Property prices, often described as the asset class of choice for urban Vietnamese and a reliable indicator of business optimism, are at an all-time high.

Hanoi may be the nation's political capital—the oldest one in Southeast Asia—but HCM City lays undisputed claim to the title of commercial and industrial capital, generating 30 percent of Vietnam's manufacturing output. (Note: Many Vietnamese still refer to HCM City as Saigon except under official circumstances. When dealing with government officials and others for the first time, however, it is best to refer to HCM City.)

In contrast to Hanoi, which is like a large town, HCM City is a sprawling, bustling place. With an official population of five million and a history of greater exposure to capitalism under the French and then the U.S., HCM City is not unlike many other large Asian cities in appearance and mentality. It is like a small province, covering nearly eight hundred square miles and extending from the South China Sea (East Sea is the politically correct term in Vietnam.) almost to the Cambodian border. Many Vietnamese from other parts of the country, as well as foreigners, see HCM City as lacking Hanoi's charm and ambience. For example, one U.S. American who has traveled to Vietnam many times to help build schools, clinics, and community development centers described HCM City as more metropolitan, businesslike, fast-paced, and developed than Hanoi. Many ambitious Vietnamese and foreigners see HCM City as the land of milk and honey, where opportunity awaits and jobs abound.

Hai Phong City, a major seaport close to the Gulf of Tonkin and about 60 miles from Hanoi, has a population of 1.8 million. Though it has only a domestic airport, it still ranks third as a destination for foreign investment. Finally, Da Nang City, located in central Vietnam, has 700,000 inhabitants. As befits a major industrial center of its stature, Da Nang has a modern seaport and airport, and is the port of entry for central Vietnam.

After reading this chapter and becoming familiar with the basic information presented here, you should now have the beginnings of a better appreciation of the country—an appreciation that will help you in developing relationships there.

As we've seen, Vietnam is a dynamic and fascinating country, a place of great diversity in its people, its climate, and its landscape. Foreign influence—on the Vietnamese language, on religious life, on the country's urban architecture, and, in some areas, even on the mind-set of the people—plays a major role in this diversity. Vietnam's economy and political system are still in flux, bringing together two very different systems to produce a uniquely Vietnamese approach to both governance and development. As you come in contact with the country of Vietnam and interact with the Vietnamese, I hope that you will find the material from this chapter helpful in providing context that will deepen your understanding.

CHAPTER THREE

A Brief History

Nothing is more precious than independence and freedom.

—Ho Chi Minh

Empires fall. Even the colonial empire came to an end. But culture remains. The Vietnamese people have lived through several such experiences in the course of their eventful history.

—Huu Ngoc

Unlike countries whose geography insulates them somewhat from foreign attack, Vietnam—which is bordered by China to the north and Laos and Cambodia to the west—has been vulnerable to invasion from land and sea throughout its history. Kieu, in the national poem *The Tale of Kieu,* symbolizes in many ways the fate of the Vietnamese and their country. In a bilingual edition of this literary masterpiece, the translator, Huynh Sanh Thong, notes that "the individual, like Kieu herself, has all too often become the toy of necessity, has been compelled to do the bidding of some alien power, to serve a master other than the one to whom he or she should owe allegiance" (Nguyen 1983, xl).

In every country, the past is prologue, and nowhere is this adage more relevant than in Vietnam. A knowledge of history is essential for an understanding of the context of contemporary thought and action. And, as many insightful foreigners have observed, Vietnam is a place where history is not an abstraction but a living, breathing entity.

History and Vietnam's "National Personality"

In *The Vietnamese and Their Revolution,* John McAlister summarizes the writings of Paul Mus, the French sociologist and one-time political adviser to France's high commissioner for Indochina. Published toward the end of the Vietnam War, the book, which made Mus's writings accessible to the English-speaking world, should be required reading for anyone interested in the influence of national history on the behavior and mindset of a people. Some of Mus's thoughts cut to the core of the Vietnamese mentality. Mus writes, "Nearly everyone agrees that the Vietnamese are energetic and tenacious workers when they are motivated, a situation which is hardly infrequent, especially for the peasants in the fields. . . . The spirit or mentality of the Vietnamese—the three-fourths of them who continue to lead the lives rooted in the traditions of the village—is the essential untold story about Viet Nam. (1970, 6)

Indeed, even most city people in Vietnam retain strong ties to the countryside and periodically make pilgrimages to the villages where they or their parents and grandparents were born to pay respects to their ancestors.

There is one main historical factor that has shaped Vietnam's character. The original Vietnamese, people of Mongoloid and Indonesian racial origin who came from what is now central and southern China, based their economy on wet rice farming, which is highly dependent on weather and on complex systems of irrigation. As a result, Vietnamese communities developed a strong collective spirit. Though administratively autonomous, each village could be quickly mobilized, along with neighboring villages, in the event of foreign invasion. This made military victory over the Vietnamese problematic. Foreign forces would literally have to win the war one village at a time, and gains were often short-lived, in contrast to other countries where the fall of a fortress might mean control of an entire city. Vietnamese history is generally seen as one of nation building and defense.

The notion of mobilizing autonomous villages to resist foreign invaders is not difficult to imagine when you see the physical layout of villages on the approach to any of the nation's major airports or while traveling through the countryside. According to the historian Stanley Karnow, Vietnam's many wars "infused in the Vietnamese a readiness to defend themselves, so that they evolved into a breed of warriors" (1983, 99). The desire to defend their country from foreign attack remains as strong as ever, but the Vietnamese are "warriors" not by their nature but only when provoked by foreign aggression. In his monumental work *Sketches for a Portrait of Vietnamese Culture,* Huu Ngoc, a self-described "cultural worker" and one of Vietnam's preeminent intellectuals, writes, with understatement, "With questions of ideology fading with the passage of time, perhaps future historians will agree among themselves that, at bottom, all that fighting was for national liberation" (1996, 262).

Chinese Rule

Châu chấu đá xe. "DAVID FIGHTS GOLIATH."

—PROVERB

In the summer of 1945, as Chinese soldiers streamed into Hanoi, ostensibly to wrest power away from the remaining Japanese according to the terms of the Potsdam Agreement, Ho Chi Minh chastised his critics at a meeting:

> You fools! Don't you realize what it means if the Chinese remain? Don't you remember your history? The last time the Chinese came, they stayed a thousand years. The French are foreigners. They are weak. Colonialism is dying. The white man is finished in Asia. But if the Chinese stay now, they will never go. As for me, I prefer to sniff French shit for five years than eat Chinese shit for the rest of my life (Karnow 1983, 153).

Both colorful and prophetic, Ho's remark is indicative of a love/hate relationship with China that spans centuries. In fact, the very name of the country refers to the majority of people, who are of "Viet" (*Kinh*) ethnic origin, *and* to the location of the country in relation to present-day China—"Nam" (south). Vietnamese culture bears the imprint of many centuries of Chinese influence, especially in the North—at times willingly accepted and emulated, at other times forcibly and cruelly imposed.

The Chinese occupied the Red River Delta in northern Vietnam for nearly a millennium, from 179 B.C. until national independence was restored in A.D. 938. The occupation was marked by economic exploitation and the transformation of Au Lac—"country of the Viets," in reference to the dominant ethnic group—from a matriarchy into a patriarchal, feudalistic society. It is said that the Vietnamese had to make payments to the occupying power in the form of ivory, sandalwood, handcrafts, and work inlaid with gold, silver, and mother-of-pearl. The Chinese also introduced Confucianism, which the Vietnamese embraced as the guiding philosophy of personal and social life.

Resistance to Chinese rule is best symbolized by the rebellion, in A.D. 40, of the Trung Sisters, a story that is etched on the mind of every Vietnamese. Two sisters, one whose husband had been murdered by the Chinese, led a revolt that forced the Chinese out of Vietnam for several years. When the Chinese returned, the sisters, choosing suicide over surrender, drowned themselves in a river. Another Vietnamese Joan of Arc, Dame Trieu, instigated a rebellion in the third century A.D.; in the sixth century, Ly Bi led a major insurrection. Vietnamese celebrate many of these uprisings in festivals to this day. In the tenth century, as a result of internal problems and distractions, Tang China was forced to recognize a local Viet as governor. After his death, power shifted to Ngo Quyen, who defeated the southern Chinese navy on the Bach Dang River, thereby ending more than a thousand years of Chinese domination.

The next four hundred years saw several more Chinese attempts to regain power. After an eleventh-century Chinese offensive, the Vietnamese general Ly Thuong Kiet wrote a poem that is considered to be the first declaration of independence ever written in Vietnam:

Over the mountains and rivers of the South reigns the Emperor
 of the South
This has been decided forever by the Book of Heaven
How dare you, barbarians, invade our soil?
Your hordes, without pity, will be annihilated!

         —HUU NGOC 1996, 366–67

In the thirteenth century, the Mongols of Kublai Khan invaded Vietnam three times and met with defeat each time.

The only other Chinese occupation was for a brief period in the fifteenth century. From 1407 to 1427, the Ming Empire pursued a policy of assimilation, forcing the people to wear Chinese clothes and adopt Chinese customs. Various artifacts of national culture, such as literary works, were destroyed, and craftsmen and intellectuals were sent to China. In the Hoan Kiem district of Hanoi lies the Lake of the Restored Sword. As legend has it, when the fifteenth-century hero Le Loi went for a boat ride, a golden turtle emerged from the water to take back the sacred sword that Heaven had given the hero to expel the Chinese Ming invaders. Many temples are dedicated to Vietnamese heroes who resisted the Chinese throughout the ages.

Ho Chi Minh, whose name means "Bringer of Light" and whose picture adorns the walls of many homes throughout Vietnam, embodies this spirit of resistance and independence. Ho was named by *Time* magazine as one of "20 people (leaders and revolutionaries) who helped define the political and social fabric of our times" in the twentieth century. In the description he wrote for *Time*, Stanley Karnow describes Ho as "an emaciated, goateed figure in a threadbare bush jacket and frayed rubber sandals." Karnow writes:

> Ho Chi Minh cultivated the image of a humble, benign "Uncle Ho." But he was a seasoned revolutionary and passionate nationalist obsessed by a single goal: independence for his country. Sharing his fervor, his tattered guerrillas vaulted daunting obstacles to crush France's desperate attempt to retrieve its empire

in Indochina; later, built into a largely conventional army, they frustrated the massive U.S. effort to prevent Ho's communist followers from controlling Viet Nam. (*www.time.com/time/time100/ leaders/profile/hochiminh.html*)

Like others of his generation who had lived in France or attended French schools in Vietnam, Nguyen Ai Quoc ("Nguyen the Patriot"), as Ho called himself at the time, learned from the West but rejected its domination. (He left Vietnam in 1911 and traveled to France, Great Britain, the U.S., China, and other countries before returning home in 1941 to lead the revolution against the French.)

Vietnam has long had an ambivalent relationship with China. Long before the French conquest, the Vietnamese had borrowed Chinese culture, institutions, ethics, and even calligraphy while resisting China's efforts to control their country. Even the language was influenced by Chinese: it is estimated that 60 to 70 percent of all words are Sino-Viet. In a graphic illustration of Vietnam's ambivalent relationship with its "big brother" to the North (and of the expression that politics makes for strange bedfellows), China supported Vietnam in its war against the U.S., only to instigate a brief but costly border war in early 1979 to punish Hanoi for its crushing defeat of the genocidal Khmer Rouge regime in Cambodia a month earlier. A park in the Dong Da district of Hanoi, where children play and adults relax, doubles as a cemetery with unmarked graves. Under the grass, flowers, and laughter are buried the bodies of thousands of Chinese soldiers from a late-eighteenth-century battle, a bittersweet reminder of how China ultimately fared in its thousand-year reign over Vietnam—and also a warning for the future.

Among individual Vietnamese, feelings about the Chinese are mixed. Some Vietnamese resist "buying Chinese" but admit that this is easier said than done. Coupled with concerns about the flood of cheap Chinese imports undermining domestic industries, there is also a recognition that some Chinese products are of higher quality. By the same token, there are those who admire China for its glorious achievements in literature and in the creative and performing arts.

The Vietnamese intellectual Huu Ngoc observed that the psychological disposition of the Vietnamese people toward China "is ambiguous and even contradictory, marked by repulsion and attraction. In the interests of self-preservation, the Vietnamese had to pay tribute to the occupiers; at the same time, they had to thwart the Chinese goal of maintaining "'a weakened or divided Viet Nam'" (Ngoc 1996, 33). Ultimately, they did not allow the Chinese to change or destroy their cultural values.

China continues to be both a positive and a negative role model for Vietnam. On one side of the coin, its ability to create a flourishing market economy with the world's highest growth rate while maintaining the primacy of the Communist Party is applauded. On the other side, China remains a force to be reckoned with, both economically and militarily.

One bone of contention is the claim by both China and Vietnam to the Spratly Islands in the potentially oil-rich area of the South China Sea (known as the "East Sea" in Vietnam). There have been occasional military confrontations, some resulting in loss of life. The strategic partnership agreed on by Vietnam and Russia in 2001 is yet another attempt to maintain a balance of power in Southeast Asia. As it has so far done with great skill and finesse, Vietnam will have to continue to walk a fine line, balancing cooperation, competition, and protection of its national interest. China will continue to loom large on Vietnam's political, economic, social, and cultural horizon.

French Subjugation

French colonialism in Vietnam, though short-lived (1859–1954) in comparison with Chinese rule, distinguished itself by its sheer brutality and contempt for the Vietnamese people and their culture. France's mission, aside from plundering and profiting from Vietnam's considerable natural resources and exploiting the country's apparently inexhaustible supply of cheap labor, was to save the Vietnamese from their own political leadership—from themselves—by "civilizing" them. The French made the mistake of seeing the Vietnamese as "big children" with limited mental capacities, and of believing that their Vietnamese enemies were no better than common criminals who lacked patriotism and dedication.

In a passage from a colonial curricular guide, French administrators' paternalistic description of their work sounds like a noble calling, emphasizing their desire "to protect the people from themselves and their own shortcomings such as gambling, excessive superstitions of all sorts and their love of chicanery which ruins both their savings and their health" (Altbach and Kelly 1984, 19). Even for those few Vietnamese who had access to the colonial education system, opportunities for promotion and advancement were limited, in keeping with the French principle that "the lowest-ranked representative of France in Indochina must receive a salary superior to that of the highest Indochinese official employed by the colonial administration. In *Understanding Vietnam,* Neil Jamieson uses the example of a Vietnamese professor who graduates from the University of Hanoi, studies in France, and returns home, only to earn less than the French janitor who cleans the classroom in which he teaches (1995, 97). The main purpose of education was to create a tiny elite of Vietnamese who could assist in the administration of their own country as a French colony. By 1945, in the twilight of French rule, 95 percent of the population was illiterate.

Some, pointing to hospitals, schools, and roads, argue that France brought Vietnam the benefits of Western civilization. But although there is some truth to this, as evidenced by the restored villas of Hanoi that are now being used as government offices, embassies, and businesses, amenities such as hospitals or schools were available only to a minority of Vietnamese, while the majority suffered from the regime's taxation policies and racial prejudice.

The transcription of the Vietnamese language in the Latin alphabet from Chinese ideographs in the seventeenth century was both a blessing and a curse. It had the net effect of severing future generations from their own national literature, written in Chinese characters, as well as from a millennium of Chinese influence (Altbach and Kelly 1984, 25). But it also had a favorable impact on literacy in the long term because it made the language easier to learn than, say, Chinese or Japanese. As in other societies, the Vietnamese language was one of the keys to preserving Vietnam's national identity. Each occupying power in turn regarded Vietnamese as inferior to its own language. Like Chinese, the French language dominated Vietnamese schools, the university, the government, business, and foreign relations.

Many older men who were educated in *lycées* (French secondary schools) and later fought against the French nevertheless openly express their admiration and affinity for French culture. The views of these Vietnamese Francophiles, some of whom were charter members of Vietnam's Communist Party, reflect the tendency to distinguish between peoples and cultures on the one hand and governments and policies on the other. One political factor that might explain Vietnamese openness to things French, according to a Frenchman who has spent much of his career in Vietnam, is the current French government's foreign policy, which is decidedly more multilateral and inclusive than those of, for example, the U.S. and Great Britain. The ways in which the Vietnamese and French cultures complement each other also offer a more positive starting point than for other Westerners. A marked French influence remains in Hanoi's architecture and cuisine (e.g., baguettes, croissants, sauces), as well as in an openness toward French culture, even among young people. Some attribute this to a Vietnamese tendency toward selective cultural borrowing—retaining only what they like most—while others point to similarities between Vietnam as a tea-sipping and France as a wine-sipping café culture. In both societies, for example, developing a relationship, whether over a cup of tea or a glass of wine, always precedes "getting down to business."

Among young people, English has now become the language of choice: French ranks a distant second among the foreign languages studied by Vietnamese high school and university students. But I have been approached by older people—in formal settings, such as a meeting, as well as informal ones, for example in a park—wanting to converse with me in French. As this older generation passes on, so too will much of this linguistic bridge to Vietnam's colonial past.

Vietnam in the Post–World War II Era

In a serendipitous convergence of historical circumstances, the three countries that ultimately had such a profound and largely negative impact on Vietnam and its people—China, France, and the U.S.—found themselves in Vietnam at the end of World War II, competing for influence, each attempting to determine the fate of this geopolitical pawn and to jockey for regional influence. For China, this was an opportunity to reclaim a politically and economically important area. For France, it was a time to consolidate its power after World War II and settle in for the long term. The U.S. was at a crossroads, with the option of supporting the fledging state. Instead, because of the Cold War politics of the day, the U.S. chose to support France as a foreign occupier in Vietnam.

On September 2, 1945, before a crowd of half a million people in Hanoi's Ba Dinh square, Ho Chi Minh proclaimed Vietnam's independence from France,* invoking the words of the U.S. Declaration of Independence—with one minor modification: "All *people* are created equal. They are endowed by their creator with certain inalienable rights; among these are life, liberty, and the pursuit of happiness." Among those in attendance were military officers from the Office of Strategic Services (OSS), the forerunner to the Central Intelligence Agency, which had provided support during and immediately after the war to Viet Minh forces—the Vietnamese guerrillas who were fighting the French in "hit-and-run" fashion.

Ho's use of the word *people* is notable in a Confucian society in which women were essentially property, belonging first to their fathers, then to their husbands, and, upon their husband's death, to their eldest sons. As Lady Borton wrote in an essay entitled "The One-Word Revolution:

---

*The surrounding context of this declaration and related events was the French and, for a shorter period of time, Japanese legacy of famine, poverty, illiteracy, and oppression. The famine of 1945, which resulted in the deaths of two million Vietnamese, was caused not by a shortage of rice but by the fact that so much of it had been exported to Japan during the war. Those who are old enough to remember speak of starving people and corpses lying in the streets of Hanoi. (Vietnam is now one of the world's leading rice-exporting countries.)

Ho Chi Minh and the U.S. 'Declaration of Independence,'" "By changing one word in his translation, Ho subtly but definitively announced to his own people and to the world a second revolution: Ho Chi Minh also declared independence for Vietnamese women" (*www.aasianst.org/ Viewpoints/borton.htm*).

Ironically, Ho and his fellow revolutionaries also found inspiration in the French Revolution, which they had studied in school, and its promise of freedom, brotherhood, and equality. As in other colonial or neocolonial regimes, they learned from the ideals espoused by the mother country, if not the policies and practices of its government.

Ho Chi Minh, that same day, also asserted Vietnam's right to enjoy freedom and independence: "The entire Vietnamese people are determined to mobilize all their physical and mental strength, to sacrifice their lives and property in order to safeguard their freedom and independence" (Duiker 2000, 323). The years that followed—and two more wars, ending with the unification of Vietnam in April 1975—proved him right.

After the president of the new Democratic Republic of Vietnam concluded his remarks, the legendary General Giap, then minister of the interior and commander-in-chief of the army, and widely viewed as one of the greatest military strategists in world history, delivered a speech in which he praised the U.S. for its contributions to "the Vietnamese fight against fascist Japan, our enemy, and so the great American Republic is a good friend of ours" (Jamieson 1995, 196).

Quotes attributed to Ho Chi Minh and General Vo Nguyen Giap in the years leading up to the crushing French defeat at Dien Bien Phu in 1954, which concluded the First Indochina War, affirm Vietnam's long-term commitment to ridding the country of foreign invaders. Ho ominously warned the French, "You can kill ten of my men for every one I kill of yours, yet even at those odds, you will lose and I will win." Similarly, General Giap spoke of fighting "ten, fifteen, twenty, fifty years, regardless of cost, until final victory" (Karnow 1983, 18). What U.S. and other military leaders later viewed as insanity was simply a protracted defense of the homeland and a commitment to winning at all costs. And, just as the French had vastly underestimated the fighting prowess and tenacity of their Vietnamese opponents, so U.S. policymakers, ignoring their own intelligence, would later write off Ho Chi Minh, though an avowed Communist, as simply a Soviet pawn and "North Vietnam" as a satellite state.

In July 1954, the Geneva Accords ended the First Indochina War in Vietnam, Laos, and Cambodia. Under the terms of the agreement, the country was to be temporarily divided into two zones at the 17th parallel until free elections could be held two years later. In 1955, however, the president of South Vietnam, Ngo Diem, convinced that Ho Chi Minh would win the elections, rejected this attempt to unite the country. This was the beginning of direct U.S. involvement in Vietnam.

American Domination

> From 1964 to 1972, the wealthiest and most powerful nation in the history of the world made a maximum military effort, with everything short of atomic bombs, to defeat a nationalist revolutionary movement in a tiny, peasant country—and failed. When the United States fought in Vietnam, it was organized modern technology versus organized human beings, and the human beings won. (Zinn 1999, 469)

In perhaps the finest novel ever written about America's early involvement in Vietnam, *The Quiet American,* Graham Greene writes about Alden Pyle, a young, idealistic American whose mission is to funnel economic aid to a "Third Force" in place of the fading French colonialists and as a counterforce to the Viet Minh. Thomas Fowler, a veteran British journalist and the narrator of the story, observes, "I never knew a man who had better motives for all the trouble he caused" (1977, 60). The recent film made from this book (which, incidentally, was shown in Vietnam) is in many respects a powerful metaphor for U.S. post–World War II foreign policy, which was firmly rooted in the so-called domino theory, the belief that Vietnam and other countries were essential battlegrounds against Communist expansion.

As the Cold War began to heat up, the U.S. picked up where the

French had left off after investing $2.5 billion and imposing an economic and commercial embargo on northern Vietnam (the Democratic Republic of Vietnam) in a failed attempt to prop up France's crumbling colonial regime, which President Kennedy later termed "our Asian Berlin." At this time, it was the French desk of the U.S. State Department's Bureau of European Affairs that was responsible for Indochina.

One clear indication that the U.S. government was lacking in expertise concerning Vietnam or Indochina was the fact that, from 1954 on, the Vietnam desk at State and the U.S. Embassy in Saigon were staffed mainly by French-speaking foreign-service officers with extensive European experience. Although they could converse with the educated elite of Saigon, their knowledge of French was not very helpful in communicating with the majority of Vietnamese living beyond the confines of the city.

In 1965, more than a hundred years after the French landed on the shores of Danang, the U.S. Marines followed in their footsteps. Within two years, the U.S. had reached a troop strength of 500,000. This embodiment of the U.S. American philosopher George Santayana's warning that "those who forget the past are condemned to relive it" marked the escalation of a war the U.S. would eventually lose. When the U.S. realized that the war was lost, its initial goal of defeating the communists of North Vietnam metamorphosed into what came to be called the Vietnamization of the war—an effort to help the U.S. ally, South Vietnam, to achieve military self-sufficiency. This meant that Vietnamese would be fighting Vietnamese with U.S. aid.

The 15 million tons of munitions that the U.S. dropped during the war, more than twice the total amount expended by the American military in all of World War II in Europe and Asia, did not achieve the desired result. The targets, both human and inanimate, proved to be elusive, and the bombing failed to weaken the resolve of the leadership and the people.

The turning point in the war came in 1968 with the Tet Offensive, a coordinated series of Viet Cong attacks in over 100 cities and towns throughout Vietnam. Although it represented a resounding defeat for the communists, the Tet Offensive dealt a devastating psychological blow to the U.S. and South Vietnamese forces, proving that they were vulnerable and that no place was safe. When Ho Chi Minh died in September 1969, the U.S. government mistakenly assumed that his death would deal a severe blow to the morale of the North Vietnamese and the Viet Cong. In fact, Uncle (*Bac*) Ho, as he is called, had just been elevated from "father's older brother" in life to a revered saint in death. In the words of Pham Xuan An, the legendary Saigon-based *Time* reporter who moonlighted as a Viet Cong colonel and had been involved in the resistance movement since 1945, "The big mistake the U.S. Americans made was not understanding the Vietnamese's history, culture, mentality. They were so sure military strength would win the war, they never bothered to learn who they were fighting" (Lamb 2002, 85).

They Called It Peace

While 58,000 U.S. soldiers perished in what Vietnamese logically refer to as the American (or U.S.) War, an estimated four million Vietnamese soldiers and civilians on both sides—10 percent of the entire population—were killed or wounded, writes Stanley Karnow in his classic work *Vietnam: A History* (1997), a companion volume to the U.S. Public Broadcasting System (PBS) series of the same name. Imagine a Vietnam Veterans Memorial fifty times as large as the one on the Mall in Washington, D.C. In any military cemetery in central Vietnam, you can walk past row after row of white tombstones with the inscription "hero"—many without human remains, some with photographs of men, forever young. The years of death—1946, 1968, 1973—reflect a country at war for nearly two generations.

The skewed demographics are obvious in the often-cited statistic that over half of the population in Vietnam is younger than 25. Equally remarkable, of the 5.6 percent of Vietnamese who are 65 years and older, only 1.9 million are men while 2.7 million are women. These statistics come alive as the visitor walks through the streets or joins the wave of motorbikes in any of Vietnam's major urban centers. The sea of young faces and, among older people, of women's faces, is striking.

To this day, the physical legacy of the war is seen in the victims of the herbicide Agent Orange, the effects of which are passed on genetically from one generation to the next. There are 150,000 children in Vietnam with hideous and debilitating birth defects that are the result of their parents' exposure to Agent Orange during the war, or of the consumption of dioxin-contaminated food and water since 1975. According to the Vietnam Victims of Agent Orange Association (VAVA), which recently filed suit in the U.S. against Monsanto Corporation, Dow Chemical, and other companies that produced defoliants, three million Vietnamese were exposed to the chemical during the war, and at least one million suffer serious health problems today.

In 2003, Dr. Arnold Schecter, an expert in dioxin contamination, sampled the soil in the area around Bien Hoa, a former U.S. military base, where significant amounts of Agent Orange were stored. He found that it contained TCCD (dioxin) levels that were 180 million times above the level set as "safe" by the U.S. Environmental Protection Agency. Whereas the 10,000 U.S. Vietnam veterans who were exposed to Agent Orange receive disability benefits of up to $1,500 a month, Vietnamese families with disabled children affected by the chemical receive the equivalent of about $5 per month.

Other legacies of the war include veterans without limbs and children who play with unexploded ordnance, sometimes resulting in loss of a limb or life. (There are an estimated 3.5 million land mines in Vietnam.) And, as in the U.S., posttraumatic stress disorder (PTSD) continues to afflict large numbers of veterans. Victory is not a balm that magically heals the psychological wounds suffered in combat.

Then there are the remaining Amerasians, now young adults, who did not have the opportunity to emigrate, either legally, under approved programs, or illegally. These "children of the dust," as the offspring of unions of U.S. soldiers and Vietnamese women are known in Vietnam, live in a no-man's-land, social pariahs in their own country, forgotten in the United States.

The lingering effects of half a century of war, combined with inept policies of a leadership that could successfully wage a long-term guerrilla war but admittedly was not wholly prepared to govern a nation, are contributing factors to Vietnam's widespread and persistent poverty. In a frank postwar conversation with Stanley Karnow, former prime minister Pham Van Dong acknowledged in the early 1980s that although Vietnam had defeated the United States, "we are plagued by problems. We do not have enough to eat. We are a poor, underdeveloped nation. Waging a war is simple, but running a country is very difficult" (Karnow 1983, 28). And in a 1989 cover story entitled "Vietnam: Hard Road to Peace," a *National Geographic* reporter travels to Vietnam (Hanoi, Hue, and HCM City) to answer one question: "How is it that these courageous, ingenious, industrious people, who in three decades of armed struggle somehow managed to achieve their aims against far mightier enemies—first France and then the United States of America—have for 14 years now failed to bring to their vast majority even a halfway decent standard of living?" (*National Geographic* 1989, 570).

Today, a response to this question can be seen everywhere you look in Vietnam. Since the advent of market reforms, which began to kick in during the 1990s and are now in full swing, Vietnamese ingenuity and industriousness are beginning to pay off. Vietnam is widely viewed by the international development community as one of the developing world's great success stories in terms of aggregate economic growth.

Forgiven and Forgotten?

Nearly three decades after the end of the war, all may seem to be forgiven and forgotten, even among members of the older generation of Vietnamese. Many have horrific memories they will take with them to their graves. But they live out their years quietly, rarely giving voice to their pain, bitterness, and sense of loss. Any remaining animosity is likely to be so muted as to be undetectable.

As one young Vietnamese put it, if you ask older people about the war, many of them will probably say, " 'Same old sad story, forget about it,' while inviting you into their home for a drink because they think the tropical sun might kill you." She continues, "But somehow, the United States should know its part in that common history book." Her point is not that U.S. Americans and others whose governments were involved in the Vietnam War should be mired in guilt but, rather, that they should be aware of and concerned about the suffering that their countries inflicted on the people and landscape of Vietnam.

A promising young Vietnamese journalist, whose father died in 2001 of a cancer that doctors suspected of being related to his exposure to Agent Orange during the war, explained one of the reasons that she conducted an interview with Lady Borton: "I wrote this article as a last effort to convince my Dad, who had always hated Americans and tried to stop me from having any kind of relationship with them, that not all Americans are our enemy. If there are no different nationalities in Heaven, then what I wrote is for others. If there are, I hope he will be able to read these lines and find a way to end his hatred."

Despite its ancient history, Vietnam is by nature and necessity a future-oriented country in which people are not prone to dwell on the past. While Vietnamese are rightfully proud of their victories over the Chinese, French, and U.S. forces, and continue to celebrate these victories in festivals and holidays, they have followed Ho Chi Minh's advice by distinguishing between peoples and their governments.

When U.S. Americans travel to Vietnam for the first time, or—in the case of veterans and others who were involved in the war—make a return visit, most want to know what the Vietnamese think of them, how they will be treated, to what extent the war is still a part of the national consciousness. One U.S. American, who admitted that his view of Vietnam was "a very Western view and exclusively about the war," acknowledged that his initial gut reaction was one of fear, wondering what might happen to him when he was alone. (Obviously, this is one piece of psychological baggage that non–U.S. Americans, with few exceptions, do not carry with them.) Thus, U.S. Americans are likely to be delighted, relieved, and perhaps somewhat puzzled to discover that hatred and hostility directed toward them as individuals are virtually nonexistent in Vietnam. For the more than half of Vietnam's population born after 1975, the American War belongs to the past, something they have heard about from their parents and grandparents, the stuff of history books and museum artifacts.

In his award-winning memoir *Catfish and Mandala: A Two-Wheeled Voyage through the Landscape and Memory of Vietnam,* Andrew X. Pham, whose family escaped from Vietnam with thousands of other boat people in one of several waves of emigration to the U.S. and other countries, tells the story of his visit to the former Demilitarized Zone (DMZ) and a conversation with one of the tour guides, Cao. Speaking of the U.S. veterans who visit, Cao says, shaking his head,

> It is very sad. I see them come here. They get very emotional. They cry. Sometimes they just walk around as though they are lost. Lost their soul, you know. I feel very sorry for them. Maybe they aren't as tough as we are.

Pham asks Cao why he thinks Vietnamese soldiers can forget more easily than American soldiers and gets this response:

> He pulls a half-grin. It is a question he must have contemplated many times. "We live here. They don't. It's like, say, you and me falling in love in with the same girl. We both had good and bad times courting her, maybe she hurt us both. I win and marry her. You go home to your country far away. After twenty years, all you have of her are memories, both the good and the bad. Me, I live with her for twenty years. I see her at her best and at her worse. We make peace with each other. We build our lives, have children, and make new history together. Twenty years and you have only memories. It is not the forgetting but the new history with the girl that is the difference between you and me." (1999, 284–85)

Most U.S. Americans remain fixated on the image of the "girl" they knew in the 1960s and 1970s, and are ignorant of the seismic changes that have occurred, especially since the late 1980s and early 1990s. Even among those Vietnamese who fought against the U.S. or were otherwise victims of the war and who harbor ill will, their criticism, if it is ever detectable, is muted and directed not against individual U.S. Americans—with the possible exception of key political leaders such as Lyndon Johnson, Henry Kissinger, Robert McNamara, and Richard Nixon—but against the policies of a U.S. government of a bygone era. The Vietnamese were well aware of many U.S. citizens' opposition to and condemnation of the war.

For its part, Vietnam has neither the luxury in terms of time and resources nor the cultural predisposition to dwell on one in a series of wars that caused the deaths and resulted in the dislocation of millions of people. (In Buddhism, pain and suffering are viewed as inseparable from life.) It is a youthful and dynamic nation of 80 million people who continue to look to the future after centuries of foreign invasion, occupation, and war. Vietnam's promise and potential are embodied in its young people born after 1975, the first in a generation to grow up in peace and, for growing numbers, relative prosperity.

After 1975

In April 1975, after the last helicopter beat a hasty retreat from the roof of the U.S. Embassy in Saigon, in advance of the approaching communist forces, the Vietnamese quickly turned their attention to the tasks at hand—punishing the "enemy" from within, as victors are prone to do in the spirit of the revolution consuming its own children, and recovering from a half-century of war. Those who were affiliated with the defeated Republic of Vietnam or the U.S. government, including former government and military officials and others opposed to Communist rule, were screened and many sent to "reeducation" camps, in some cases for years. Others were marginalized and effectively prevented from participating in the new order. Many who could have made significant contributions to Vietnam's development ended up living abroad in the Vietnamese diaspora.

The Socialist Republic of Vietnam was officially created in 1976, and the new government subsequently confiscated privately owned land and collectivized agriculture. From the perspective of the U.S. government, Vietnam vanished from the political and economic radar screen in 1975, except for sporadic attempts to punish the country that had humiliated them. Political maneuvering effectively isolated Vietnam from the international community and forced the Vietnamese to rely mainly on themselves and their patron, the Soviet Union.

In 1979, the U.S. backed a Chinese invasion of Vietnam in which the Chinese destroyed three provincial capitals. That same year, the U.S. drew its European allies into an even stricter trade and aid embargo against Vietnam, which included a ban on commercial and financial transactions and on private investment, as well as a freeze on unified Vietnam's assets in the U.S. The embargo had the devastating effect of blocking Vietnam's access to the world's largest markets and to multilateral bank loans. Only with the final withdrawal of Vietnamese troops from Cambodia in 1989 did Europe and Japan end their support for the embargo. The U.S. followed suit in 1994 under the Clinton administration.

To this day, there are political sensitivities and a high level of paranoia in Vietnam's officialdom concerning the intentions and actions of the U.S. government and U.S. American NGOs. The latter include some overseas Vietnamese organizations whose goal it is to undermine and overthrow the Vietnamese government. At the same time, there are attempts by the Vietnamese government, sometimes successful, to reach out to overseas Vietnamese by appealing to their patriotism and love for their homeland. There are also prewar relationships between family members, colleagues, and teachers and students that transcend politics and have survived to this day.

U.S. American NGOs are placed in a separate category from those of other countries because of Vietnam's history with the U.S. As a "special case," these NGOs are under greater scrutiny and are more vulnerable to the shifting political winds between the two countries than are other foreign NGOs, which generally enjoy greater trust.

This distrust can also be seen in the treatment of some Vietnamese students who choose to study in the U.S. Currently, over 20,000 of Vietnam's brightest young people are studying overseas—about 10 percent of them in the U.S. and the rest in Australia, Canada, Germany, the Netherlands, the U.K., and other countries. Those who are able to study in the U.S. must give considerable thought to the possible detrimental impact of their experience on future promotion, especially if they are in the social sciences and wish to work for the government. Instead of being welcomed with open arms and reintegrated into a system that desperately needs their knowledge and experience, some Vietnamese graduates of U.S. institutions of higher education may find themselves underemployed and put on a form of ideological probation until they prove themselves. (For more discussion of this topic, see the section, "Education and Training" in Chapter 4.)

Then there is the issue of "peaceful evolution," the official term for a supposedly gradual attempt on the part of external enemies to undermine the Socialist Republic of Vietnam. Public statements by U.S. politicians about Vietnam's human rights record and religious freedom are particularly odious to the Vietnamese government and are seen as interference in Vietnam's internal affairs. From a Vietnamese perspective, the inclination is to err on the side of caution and ensure stability at all costs. Given that the relationship between the two countries has only recently begun to improve, this is to be expected.

While other countries, including Australia, Belgium, Canada, Denmark, France, Germany, Japan, Sweden (the first to normalize relations, in 1969), and the U.K., have played a pivotal role in the development of postwar Vietnam, the U.S. was a relative latecomer. The thaw in the relationship between the U.S. and Vietnam basically coincided with the withdrawal of Vietnam from Cambodia in 1989 and with official cooperation in finding U.S. American MIAs in the early 1990s.

The past decade has witnessed a flurry of activity that has gradually brought the two former adversaries closer together. Vietnamese and U.S. citizens have come to know one another through academic exchanges, government programs, business relationships, study-abroad programs, the work of nonprofit organizations, and a rapidly growing Vietnamese student presence in the U.S. President Bill Clinton's November 2000 trip to Vietnam marked the pinnacle in a process of healing and reconciliation that began in 1992 with the opening of an office in Hanoi charged with MIA search operations, the lifting of the trade embargo in 1994, and the normalization of diplomatic relations in 1995.

Just 29 years ago, Vietnam was picking up the pieces of a bloody and costly war with the United States. In Vietnam, whose people and environment bore the brunt of the war's devastation, English is now the most popular foreign language, and young people are eager to learn about the U.S. and other countries. Even the U.S. flag has become a chic fashion statement, used as a marketing ploy to increase sales of hats, bandannas, and other clothing items. U.S. and other multinational corporations are well represented in a new economic order marked by greater economic and personal freedom and more openness to the West. Battles are now being fought between Pepsi and Coca-Cola, and in other peaceful arenas, for the loyalty of brand-conscious Vietnamese consumers. U.S. and other Western-country NGOs are also key players in Vietnam's development.

There is also greater acceptance of overseas Vietnamese. Many of the 2.5 million are the political and economic refugees of the former South Vietnam, who fled their home country in several waves of immigration, illegal and officially sanctioned. They are now a major source of income to Vietnam, amounting to over $2 billion a year in family remittances, mainly from the U.S., as well as a valuable human resource among those who have returned to do business for the short or long term. One Vietnamese American, a consultant for a major international lending agency, is an economic adviser to officials at the highest levels of government. Another is the executive director of the Vietnam Education Foundation (VEF), an independent federal agency that awards fellowships to some of Vietnam's most intellectually gifted young people to pursue advanced graduate study in technical fields in the U.S.

The notion that the U.S. should know its part in the "common history book," however, while anathema to many U.S. Americans, is crucial for those who wish to develop positive relationships with the Vietnamese. This does not mean that those Westerners whose governments (e.g., Australia, New Zealand, Spain) supported the war effort in thought, word, or deed should feel guilty or accountable for the past mistakes of their governments. Rather, they should be aware of and honestly acknowledge the role that the U.S. and other foreign powers played in bringing about human suffering and environmental destruction on a grand scale on the one hand, and forging the sense of unity, national pride, and independence of which Lady Borton spoke, on the other.

In the 2001 World Values Survey, which included Vietnam for the first time, 98 percent of all Vietnamese were united in their willingness to fight for their country should there be another war, one indication of their strong national identity and pride. (Only the U.S. expressed the same level of national allegiance.) This realization will form the foundation of an enduring relationship anchored in mutual respect and equality.

Those Westerners whose countries have no connection to the war should simply be aware of the pervasive influence of Vietnam's long and tragic history on the values, beliefs, and mentality of the Vietnamese of today. Regardless of how one feels about the current system of government, the reality is that Vietnam is a free and independent country, in control of its own destiny and making every effort to become a member in good standing of the international community. There is also the sense that the government actually cares about the people it exists to serve, despite the widespread corruption and abuse of power that are recognized as problems even by the official media. This is in contrast to other countries, whose elites often use their power primarily as a means of accumulating more power and wealth at the expense of their people.

In the end, most Vietnamese will judge you not on the basis of politics, but on how well you understand Vietnamese culture and can use that understanding to your and your Vietnamese partners' advantage. An expat cited his familiarity with Vietnamese history as the important lesson he had learned: that millions of Vietnamese died in the war with the U.S., that it wasn't just about communism but about unification and the fact that they had fought the Chinese for over a thousand years and the French for a hundred years. A basic knowledge of the ebb and flow of Vietnamese history, and an appropriate and subtle demonstration of that knowledge, will send the positive message that you are sincerely interested in Vietnam and its people.

CHAPTER FOUR

Vietnam at Peace

Cái khó ló cái khôn.
"Poverty is the mother of invention / Adversity is a great
teacher."

—Proverb

Buôn có bạn bán có phuờng.
"Traders never want to be alone in the market. They all seek
mutual cooperation to achieve success in business."

—Proverb

In this chapter, we focus on some of the defining issues and trends in
Vietnam today. The descriptions of Vietnam that follow, taken from the
foreign affairs websites of four Western countries, reflect each country's
current (as of 2004) view and policy toward Vietnam. As we shall see,
these descriptions reflect each country's foreign policy: some are more
accurate and more objective than others; some are more responsive than
others to the needs and aspirations of the developing world. An additional factor is the history between Vietnam and the governments from
whom the information is taken. All four descriptions, however, reflect
commonly held views of Vietnam as perceived by four major Western
governments.

Vietnam is a poor but developing agrarian country controlled by
a communist government. Tourist facilities are not well established,

but are improving in certain areas, especially in Hanoi and HCMC and several beach and mountain resorts.

Vietnam is a one-party state, with the Communist Party as the dominant political force. The past decade has seen a period of *doi moi*, or renovation, in Vietnam, which has led to remarkable improvements in the nation's economy, and significant improvements in quality of life for many Vietnamese.

Since the early 1990s, Vietnam's economy has been in transition from a planned economy to a market economy "with socialist orientation." This incremental policy of "renovation" resulted in remarkable economic successes in the first years of its implementation, including a high economic growth rate and large increases in exports. At the same time, structural problems have become apparent in recent years, leading to the restructuring of state companies, the modernization of the financial and banking sectors and the establishment of an efficient bureaucracy and legal structures.

Vietnam is one of the world's five remaining one-party communist states. Decision-making in Vietnam is shared by national and provincial government and agencies, slowing the political process and encouraging a cautious approach to major policy issues. Political power lies with the Communist Party of Vietnam. Its peak organ, the fifteen-member Politburo, holds authority over the implementation of social, economic, labour, defence, security and foreign policy. . . .

The first description, from the U.S. State Department, seems quaint by present-day standards. It may have applied to the Vietnam of the 1980s, but it bears only a faint resemblance to the Vietnam of 2004. The other descriptions—from the embassy websites of Canada, Germany, and Australia, respectively—are more informative, accurate, and comprehensive. In short, they do justice to the progress that Vietnam has made without sidestepping or whitewashing the many problems or challenges that it faces.

Vietnam is one of the fastest changing societies in the world. Some of these changes are reflected in the 2001 World Values Survey conducted in Vietnam and sixty-four other countries, representing 80 percent of the world's population. This study, which was conducted under the direction of Professor Pham Minh Hac, director of the Institute for Human Studies in Hanoi, in cooperation with the Center for the Study of Democracy at the University of California in Irvine, spanned a number of key areas, including subjective well-being, social relationships, family values, ethics and religion, economics, and politics. As the authors acknowledge, even Vietnam's participation in the World Values Survey is a reflection of these changes.

Here are some relevant and interesting results:

On subjective well-being:

- Nearly all Vietnamese (91 percent) say they are very or quite happy with their situation; about two-thirds rate themselves as satisfied with life overall.
- These statistics place Vietnam above most of the developing world and on a par with nations such as China, Mexico, Chile, and Spain.
- Most people score themselves as satisfied with their financial status.

On social relationships:

- The family is the most important social structure in Vietnamese society. The family also is the center of social life: most Vietnamese report weekly contact with parents or other relatives.
- Work is also an important focus for social life. One-third say they have weekly contact with work colleagues, and more than half say work is important in their lives.
- Most Vietnamese are skeptical of their fellow human beings: 59 percent say that one needs to be careful in dealing with other people. Still, this level of social trust is higher than in most other nations at Vietnam's level of economic development.

On family values:

- Most Vietnamese (99 percent) think that parents are to be respected regardless of their qualities and faults. A full 97 percent also state that "one of my main goals in life has been to make my parents proud."
- Most people (88 percent) believe that family life deserves more emphasis.
- Nearly everyone (91 percent) rejects the view that marriage is an outdated institution. Most respondents (97 percent) agree that both husband and wife should contribute to household income.
- Belief in a traditional role for women remains strong. A large majority say that a woman needs to have children (86 percent) and that housework is as fulfilling as working for pay (86 percent). A majority (56 percent) also think that men are better suited than women for politics.

On economics:

- Reflecting the economic reforms of the last decade, the broad majority now favor private ownership of businesses (81 percent) over government ownership (19 percent).
- Even if the market economy is not fully functional, answers to a variety of questions indicate that the values of market competition are generally endorsed.
- The work ethic is very strong in Vietnam. Many people say that work is an important part of their lives, and less attention is paid to leisure as a pursuit.

These statistics tell the story of a society in rapid economic, political, and social transition. Vietnam is also a country that has managed to maintain a high degree of stability and consistency through extended periods of upheaval. The need to make a living and the struggle for existence can be seen in the predominance of a strong work ethic and in the attitude toward leisure. Very few Vietnamese (7 percent) say that leisure is important, contrasted with a sizable percentage of Japanese (40 percent) and U.S. Americans (43 percent). The support for privately owned businesses reflects both official policy and current reality. Nevertheless, most Vietnamese prefer to work for a state-owned company, a holdover from the old command economy that offered job security and predictability, if not a high salary. Not surprisingly, there remains a very strong emphasis on the family and family life as the most important social unit and activity for most Vietnamese. The Vietnamese retain their strong sense of national identity and pride.

In a survey conducted by the British market research company TNS Vietnam, Vietnam's urban residents were very optimistic about 2004, the Year of the Monkey. Of those surveyed in Hanoi and HCM City, more than 80 percent predicted that this year would be better than 2003. Nearly three-quarters felt secure about their jobs and expected 2004 to bring more economic prosperity. Reflecting regional differences related to business, 43 percent of HCM City residents surveyed had "strong business aspirations," compared with 28 percent in Hanoi.

Economic Reforms

> Mạnh ai nấy chạy. "Everyone for himself."
>
> —Proverb

> "You open the window and get fresh air; you also get flies and mosquitoes."
>
> —Expatriate Vietnamese

As we discussed in the preceding chapter, a combination of factors contributed to the poverty of Vietnam in the postwar era, including two generations of war, subsequent conflicts with the Khmer Rouge in Cambodia and with the Chinese, the crippling effects of the U.S.-led trade embargo, and the country's rigid command economy. Consistent with the priorities and goals of a centrally planned economy, the state owned the major means of production, allocated resources, determined production quotas, and set prices. Real GDP growth slowed to just over 4 percent in 1978, the same year in which a food shortage occurred because of slumping agricultural production. Industrial production actually showed a negative growth rate between 1978 and 1980.

In an effort to reverse this trend, at the Fifth Plenum, in July 1979, the Central Committee announced a new set of economic policies intended to encourage private production and the sale of some commodities not under state control. In the agricultural sector, farmers were permitted to cultivate land not in use by the cooperatives and were given more freedom to sell their surplus on the open market. Because of the rapid increase in the money supply and the cost of the reforms, however, food shortages persisted and inflation continued to rise.

Against this backdrop of hyperinflation, food shortages, and structural imbalances in the economy, at the Sixth Party Congress, in December 1986, the government introduced a comprehensive reform program known as *doi moi* ("renovation"). The objectives of the reforms, which led to what is officially known as a "market economy with socialist orientation," were as follows:

- To develop the private sector
- To increase and stabilize agricultural output
- To shift the focus of investment from heavy to light industry
- To reduce the role of state enterprises
- To focus on export-led growth, following the path of some of Vietnam's regional neighbors
- To attract foreign direct investment, seen as essential for economic development

Other goals were more openness to the West, a greater acceptance of overseas Vietnamese, and increased personal freedom.

The decade of the 1990s, when the effects of the reforms first became visible and Vietnam welcomed companies from around the world, was a time of high expectations and rapid growth. There was a feeling of exuberance and unbridled optimism, a sense among the pioneers—both Vietnamese and foreign—that everything was possible in this virgin capitalist economy. It was also a decade of adjustment, transition, and learning for the Vietnamese, many of whom had never before experienced a market economy, as well as for the government and the Party, which now had to learn new lessons and become attuned to the dynamics of a market economy. (Recall the Western businessman in Chapter 1 who had to train all of his local employees except the driver.)

It wasn't until the U.S. rescinded its trade embargo in 1994, however, that Vietnam's economy really began to take off. When I first went to Vietnam in 1996, I encountered cities abuzz with economic activity. With each subsequent visit—with the exception of 1997, when Vietnam caught a case of the Asian economic "flu" and the bottom fell out of the real estate market and slowed the construction boom—I noticed more businesses, buildings, advertising, and competition.

In 2001, a constitutional amendment was passed that gives the private sector parity with state-owned enterprises. And, as the 2001 World Values Survey revealed, the vast majority of Vietnamese at least pay lip service to a preference for privately owned over state-owned companies. In 2002, overall industrial production rose by over 14 percent, driven in part by growing consumer affluence, which translates into steadily increasing sales of cars, motorbikes, and various home and electronic appliances. Industrial output by the private sector grew by almost 20 percent in 2002 and now accounts for almost 40 percent of industrial production. Vietnam's GDP recorded a growth rate of well over 7 percent in 2003, the second highest in Asia after China. Business and foreign investor confidence continue to increase.

According to Andy Gent, chief executive officer of HSBC (the Hong Kong Shanghai Banking Corporation) in Vietnam, HSBC saw more interest in Vietnam during the first six months of 2003 than in the previous six years. This is explained in part by the ratification of a bilateral trade agreement (BTA) with the U.S., which has resulted in the opening of a major new export market in industries that had to contend with high import tariffs in the past. The Vietnamese garment sector, in particular, appears to have benefited greatly from the BTA, with local and foreign-invested garment companies alike upgrading their operations to keep pace with new orders from the U.S. Before the BTA, I recall seeing Vietnamese-manufactured shirts and other clothing items only in Canada and other countries outside the U.S. Now the "Made in Vietnam" label is everywhere in the U.S.

The southern provinces are the disproportionate contributors to and beneficiaries of economic success. In a joint 2004 report entitled "History of Policy: Why Don't Northern Provinces Grow Faster," the Vietnamese Central Institute for Economic Management and the United Nations Development Programme (UNDP) found that four southern provinces, with only half the population of the northern seven, created 209,000 jobs, triple the figure for the northern provinces. The reasons for this include the North's history, lack of experience with a market economy, difficulty dealing with foreign and domestic private investors, and a tendency to look to large state-operated enterprises to set the tone. Among the recommended solutions to this problem are regional efforts to increase competitiveness, including improving the performance of business associations, and national leadership emanating from Hanoi and HCM City that rewards provinces that develop competitive industry, rather than maintaining a costly and inefficient subsidized system.

The country's economic growth, as measured statistically, appears all the more impressive because of the very modest starting point. But the fact is that Vietnam, with an annual per capita income of under $500, remains one of the poorest countries in the world. The monthly income of those in Vietnam's state sector in 2003 was 1.2 million Vietnamese *dong* (VND), or $76. The range in non-state firms and foreign-owned companies was $22–$51 and $51–$205, respectively. In part, this explains the widespread practice of "moonlighting" in order to make ends meet, to improve one's standard of living, to pay for a child's education, or, for some people, simply to "keep up with the Nguyens."

Corruption and Bureaucracy

Corruption—considered by many, including government and Party leaders, to be one of the country's most pressing problems—affects foreigners and Vietnamese alike. In the late 1980s, the Vietnamese government began trimming its subsidies to government offices, which created the need for "commissions" in order to supplement a paltry state salary that was inadequate to meet basic needs.

Upon mutual agreement with a foreign partner, a Vietnamese office may take a management fee; this is an auditable, above-board expense. However, each bureaucratic level handling funds may also take a "silent fee"—and these are nonauditable, below-board costs. For some neophytes, the first indication that silent fees have been paid comes when all of the money has been spent, yet the factory is still roofless. One expatriate international NGO colleague describes this potential slippage as similar to moving a fifty-kilo block of ice from Hanoi to HCM City in July: you're lucky to arrive with a damp spot (Borton 2001, 22).

Transparency International's (*www.transparency.org*) 2001 Perceptions Index reflects the degree to which corruption is perceived to exist among public officials and politicians and ranks ninety-one countries using scores from 1 to 10. Some of the world's richest countries, including Finland, Denmark, New Zealand, Iceland, Singapore, and Sweden, scored 9 or higher, indicating very low levels of perceived corruption. Fifty-five countries, many of the world's poorest, scored less than 5. In many cases, the corruption is linked to poverty and power relationships in that society. Vietnam ranks seventy-fifth, with Zambia, and just below Honduras, India, Kazakhstan, and Uzbekistan. It's important, however, to take into account that some practices that are defined as corruption in Western countries could be considered a cost of doing business in Vietnam.

Companies are advised to adhere to transparent management practices, meaning that they should properly maintain all files, budgets, reports, audits, minutes, correspondence, and other records. As one expatriate with ten years of in-country experience observed, there are too many secrets and not enough transparency in a system of evolving legal, financial, and regulatory systems, inflexible labor laws, and a lack of freedom of information. There also are not enough qualified people to enforce those laws that are on the books.

One classic example from the gray area of corruption is that of a government office that receives a contract from a development organization or international lending agency to provide a car with a driver, interpreters, computers, and other logistical support to a small group of consultants. The government office then enters into the same arrangement with one foreign agency or organization after another, while billing each organization the same amount. The end result is a rather substantial profit from what appears to be a "clean transaction," official receipts and all.

One expatriate who has been offered large amounts of money to perform various favors addresses this dilemma as follows: he offers advice and assistance to the people with whom he is working, and perhaps to their family members—but not money. On occasion, he will even hire family members, which is not unusual in Vietnam, but only those who are qualified for the position. With this approach, he has established a reputation as someone of integrity who cannot be "bought." As he cautions, once you head down the slippery slope of corruption by paying one person a bribe, word gets around and you end up paying everyone, with unsatisfactory or even no results.

In another example, a woman who was leading a tour to a Western country requested a foreigner's assistance because of a visa denial. To sweeten the deal, she offered him $25,000, which he promptly rejected. He promised to help anyway, but without any money changing hands. In another case, a government official who earns 1 million VND a month (about $64 US) asked this same expatriate to deposit $300,000 into a Western bank account. The expat declined, joking that it would take the Vietnamese man nearly four hundred years to earn that much money legitimately.

Among foreigners, chronic complaining about Vietnam's "bureaucracy" is often code for "Things don't work as efficiently or as quickly as they do at home" or "Why is it taking so long for the Vietnamese to make a decision?" But although bureaucracy and red tape do exist in Vietnam, this is not a uniquely Vietnamese phenomenon. There are also other invisible forces at work that are related to decision-making style, as we will discuss in Chapter 6.

Education and Training

#1 Rule: Teachers are always right.
#2 Rule: If not, see rule #1.

—Vietnamese graduate student

Together with economic changes in the transition period,
the educational system in Viet Nam needs changing as it is
out-of-date and has not been able to stimulate the full
participation of learners and make full use of the mental
and creative capacity of students. The learning process is still
too passive and inclined to one-way communication.

—Vietnamese graduate student

With typically Vietnamese understatement, these comments sum up some of the major challenges facing Vietnam's education system as it attempts to keep pace with the economic reforms of the past fifteen years. The second statement, written several years ago by a Vietnamese applicant in an admissions essay for a U.S. graduate program, now forms the centerpiece of the debate over education raging even in the country's official media. In a February 2004 article, "Education Reform Urgent: Overseas Student," *Viet Nam News* quoted three people: Trinh Thanh Tam, a Vietnamese student at Cornell University; Vo Tong Xuan, the rector of An Giang University in the Mekong Delta; and Luong The Vinh, who studied at the Hanoi Teacher Training University's Mathematics and Informatics Specialized School.

Some of their criticisms?

- Students are expected to take notes passively on everything teachers say and to learn everything without the benefit of conducting their own research.
- The curriculum relies too much on theory, without enough hands-on experience.
- Science classes rely exclusively on textbooks.

- History classes are based entirely on rote learning.
- Math textbooks include problems that are either "too easy or bizarrely complicated."
- Literature classes are taught using "dull analysis."
- Teachers are unwilling to change their teaching style and techniques.
- English textbooks date back to 1985.

Many high school students complain about a lack of motivation, insufficient time for extracurricular activities, fatigue, boredom, and a crushing workload. Another complaint, not uncommon in exam-driven systems, is that most forget what they learned soon after they take an examination.

A young Vietnamese who earned a high-level degree in a social sciences discipline from a foreign university returned to a position in English as a Foreign Language (EFL). His teaching responsibilities included five classes with up to forty students in each. He lamented, "There are so many problems with the system here. I came back realizing how difficult it is even if you have a good heart. That's not enough. We all work hard and try to make the courses beneficial to the students. We are using a very old book from the time I was a student (a long, long time ago)."

As a Confucian society, Vietnam has always placed a high value on education. The Temple of Literature in Hanoi, built in 1076 in honor of Confucius and his disciples, is the site of the country's first university. One of the very first actions of the government in 1945 was to initiate a literacy campaign that ultimately resulted in a literacy rate of 94 percent, an astounding feat in the midst of war, poverty, and dislocation.

According to Confucian ethics, the teacher–student relationship supersedes that of father–son. What Westerners may interpret as passivity among Vietnamese students who seem reluctant to participate reflects a Confucian respect toward their teacher. In a collectivist society like Vietnam, in which individuals generally shy away from standing out in the crowd, this apparent passivity is also the actualization of the notion that "the nail that sticks up gets hammered down" and the belief that to risk failure in a group setting is to risk losing face among your peers.

Given the youthfulness of the population and the close link between any society's education system and its economy, education will be one of the highest policy and fiscal priorities of the state and the Party for the foreseeable future. With 1.5 million young people entering the workforce every year, it is imperative that the system provide high-quality education and training that will meet the needs of the labor market. The alternative is growing dissatisfaction, disaffection, and possibly instability. There is increasing recognition that, in addition to fiscal commitment, some cultural adjustments will also be needed in order to create an education system that is more up-to-date and better able to "stimulate the full participation of learners and make full use of the mental and creative capacity of students."

Vietnam is a country in which inspirational stories abound—stories of tragedy, hardship, and obstacles overcome. There is the young woman, working for an international NGO, who was born into a poor and large family. Her father worked as a cyclo driver and her mother sold green tea on the street, but despite their hard work and many sacrifices, they could not afford to send all of their children to school. This young woman's older sister, who was an outstanding student, had to drop out of high school for financial reasons. One of her brothers, who attended school only through the fourth grade, later became a heroin addict and died after serving out a two-year prison sentence for stealing money to buy drugs. In a scholarship application the young woman writes,

> All of these experiences in my family have inspired me to continue my studies because I believe that better education will help increase my understanding of the social problems that have affected my family and others like us. This will enable me to find a better way to help others who have fewer opportunities than me to avoid and solve their problems.

This story has a happy ending: the young woman was awarded a full scholarship to pursue a degree at a prestigious foreign institution. She will return to Vietnam with the ideal marriage of experience and formal education that will enable her to continue a promising career in the field of community development and in the service of Vietnam's rural poor.

Primary and Secondary Education

In 2003, the government of Vietnam issued a decree on family planning that sets no limit on the number of children couples can have. This will likely lead to an increase in the birthrate for the foreseeable future, which in turn will have long-term implications for the education system. Vietnam has been successful in universalizing primary education and aims to make lower secondary education universal in the next twenty years.

In Vietnam, children begin primary school at age six. The main curricular emphasis is on the development of language and mathematics skills, and on civics. Lower secondary education, grades six through nine, features a standardized curriculum that offers virtually no elective courses. The high-priority subjects in terms of weekly hours are mathematics, a foreign language, Vietnamese, and literature. Students take exams at the end of each academic year, and, in order to attend high school, they must pass an admissions exam.

At the completion of upper secondary school, students who wish to continue their education must take a demanding national entrance examination. As in other countries with elite higher education systems and a battery of exit and entrance examinations, entering an institution of higher education is exceedingly difficult and stressful for most high school students and virtually impossible for ethnic-minority students and those from rural areas. One of our Vietnamese respondents observed:

> Every parent wants their child to go to a university. They do everything, sacrifice everything to achieve this goal. If you go to Vietnam from April to June, you will see thousands of students with their heads buried in piles of books preparing for the university entrance exam. Many of my friends who could not pass this horrible exam wanted to commit suicide. One did. It was too late and we lost him forever.

Once a student is admitted, however, the path to graduation is said to be relatively smooth and easy.

Higher Education

Since the early 1990s, Vietnamese higher education has experienced an explosion of demand that neither the state sector nor the more recently established "people-founded" (private) institutions can realistically hope to meet. (The use of the phrase *people-founded* is an example of political semantics, reflecting an aversion to the word *private*, with its overtones of capitalism.)

The Confucianist value that places a premium on education naturally extends to higher education; a university degree is thought to lead to more respect, more money, and a better life. As one Vietnamese colleague observed, "Everyone wants to become a boss," with the appropriate degree and title. It is the job applicants with the best credentials and the highest grades who get hired. In a sense, it is like a game that people are obliged to play: enroll in a relatively inexpensive degree or certificate program, jump through the requisite hoops, and walk away with your credential. One by-product of the economic reforms in the education sector has been rampant credential fraud.

Between 1992 and 1995, the number of students attending Vietnamese universities more than doubled, from 210,000 to 414,000, doubling again between 1995 and 1997. Enrollments of first-year students rose to 197,000 in 2003, an increase of 7 percent—a rate of growth that is expected to continue until 2010. With only about 150 universities and colleges in Vietnam, serving nearly a million students, the result is a higher education system with low faculty salaries, crumbling infrastructure, overcrowding, outdated curriculum and training, and mixed results in its efforts to produce graduates who have the skills and qualifications needed to prosper in the new economy.

Although Vietnam also has a system of vocational education, it is not viewed in a positive light, as it is in some Western countries, particularly in Europe. One common theme is that Vietnam's higher education system is unable to meet current and projected demand, while at the same time it produces graduates who end up underemployed because there is a disjuncture between the economy's needs and what institutions of higher education are offering. A graduate of one of Vietnam's national universities painted this rather bleak picture:

> The vocational training system in Vietnam is waiting to die because most of the students don't want to go there to study if they fail the university entrance exam. Studying in a vocational school means you're a loser. MOET [the Ministry of Education and Training] has failed to convince young people that Vietnam now needs good skilled workers much more than redundant university graduates.

Grades in Vietnam's colleges and universities are based on the final exam, which means that most students tend to procrastinate until the end of the semester, just one or two weeks before, or even during, the final exam period. Generally, students do not care how they perform during the semester as long as they do well on the final exams. Most classes use only one textbook. Standards for faculty are also problematic: instructors do not necessarily obtain the rank of professor on merit but, rather, primarily on the basis of how many books they have published, regardless of quality. As a result, universities often end up with professors who are not as knowledgeable as they should be about the subject they are teaching.

Most universities and colleges are monodisciplinary institutions based on the Soviet model, with no connection between teaching and research. Consequently, students, too, are not required to do any research. A graduate of one institution that specializes in international trade described his program as good because it is very specialized and detailed. It uses a step-by-step approach to teach students how to deal with export/import and related matters such as insurance and transportation.

The omnipotence of the professor, low salaries, and intense pressure to achieve high grades in order to get a good job all foster several unsavory practices. Teachers are regarded as always correct, so there is little or no debate in classrooms. Many students need to take extra classes or lessons in order to get higher grades. Finally, it is common practice for a student simply to slip his professor an envelope full of money before an exam to ensure a good grade without having to study too much or to ensure "fairness" if he does study hard for the exam.

By contrast, there are some innovative new programs that incorporate the latest teaching methodologies, the best materials available, and high-quality teaching. I once made a presentation to the students of one such program and was impressed by the high degree of interaction and the many questions they asked. This same program asks its students to evaluate their instructors after every class; the instructors do the same, using very specific criteria and making the feedback available to students in computerized form.

Nonpublic Higher Education

In 1989, not long after the government had implemented the 1986 economic reforms, Vietnam's first nonpublic higher education institution, as it was called, was founded. There are two different types of nonpublic educational institutions:

1. Semipublic (*ban cong*) facilities are owned and operated by the state and a public authority at the central, provincial, district, or commune level. All operating costs are covered by student fees.
2. People-founded (*dan lap*) institutions are owned and managed by NGOs or private associations such as trade unions, cooperatives, youth organizations, and women's associations. They are similar to semipublic institutions in that there is full cost recovery.

In 2002–2003, Vietnam had a total of twenty-three nonpublic higher education institutions, including sixteen people-founded universities, one semipublic university, two people-founded colleges, and four semipublic colleges. Most nonpublic institutions (ten universities and all colleges) are located in HCM City.

The first and only foreign-owned university campus, created by the Royal Melbourne Institute of Technology (Australia), opened in the fall of 2003 in HCM City. Another Australian institution, Swinburne University of Technology, is investing in a campus in Ba Ria-Vung Tau, a province south of that city. In addition, a number of French public universities are working with overseas Vietnamese private investors to establish another private university in HCM City in 2004. Given the current interest in investing in higher education, there may soon be a third type of nonpublic institutions, private (*tu nhan*) institutions that are fully owned and managed by private individuals. These schools, which will not have to offer the usual ideological courses, will thereby have more room in the curriculum for practical subjects.

Nonpublic institutions, offering majors in high-demand subjects like English, business, management, computer science, and technology, have proved to be an effective alternative means of increasing access to higher education in Vietnam. They account for more than 20 percent of the total number of the nation's institutions of higher education, and accommodate one-tenth of its students.

There is not yet a full system of legal documents stipulating the precise relationship between nonpublic institutions and the Ministry of Education and Training (MOET). Since 1993, when the first nonpublic university was officially established, MOET has issued only one regulation covering people-founded institutions. The lack of a regulative framework and an accreditation system has adversely affected public confidence in the nonpublic sector. Administrators at a number of nonpublic universities and colleges have abused their power, taking financial advantage of both students and their parents. As one example, Taiwan Asian International University (AIU), established in 1995 in cooperation with Hanoi University of Foreign Languages, was revealed to be a hoax after five years of operation, leaving more than two thousand students and their families with no place to go after losing of hundreds of thousands of dollars. This incident led to the removal of the MOET vice minister. In another incident involving a nonpublic institution of higher learning, Dong Do University recruited twice as many students as its capacity allowed (Le and Ashwill 2004).

Clearly, there is a need to require nonpublic institutions of higher education to be subject to routine auditing and to submit transparent annual financial reports. In addition, there should be a healthy competition between public and nonpublic higher education institutions for government grants. While public institutions are encouraged to carry out entrepreneurial activities to increase their revenue, it is unfair to leave nonpublic institutions entirely on their own while in fact they are easing the burden of excessive demand on the state.

As in other sectors of Vietnamese society, the system of laws, regulations, and oversight is still developing. Meanwhile, abuses in private higher education have come at the hands of those who see this as a lucrative market to be tapped and a valuable commodity to be sold to the highest bidder.

Foreign Study

Since the early 1990s, many parents and students have looked longingly toward the quality, prestige, and credibility associated with an overseas degree. Prior to 1992, top-notch students were awarded scholarships on a competitive basis to study economics, math, physics, chemistry, philosophy, literature, and other subjects in the Soviet Union, East Germany, Hungary, Poland, and Czechslovakia, among other socialist countries. But MOET reports that in 1992 Vietnam sent only 112 students abroad.

The surging popularity of foreign study is the result of several converging political, social, and economic forces. As the country's economic reforms began to take hold, they worked their magic, generating wealth among the nation's urban elite and increasing demand for a quality higher education that would be relevant to the needs of a market economy. The increased availability of information gleaned from contact with foreigners, Internet access, and returning graduates was a contributing factor. Finally, the government's de facto laissez-faire policy toward overseas study and travel was another catalyst.

Since 1992, Vietnamese students have had the freedom to study abroad without government control. They apply for a passport from the Ministry of Public Security and then for a student visa from the respective embassy. Of the thousands of Vietnamese students who are now going abroad each year, most pursue undergraduate degrees in Australia, Canada, Japan, New Zealand, the United Kingdom, and the United States. Ironically, in a country that prides itself on control of information and people, this system has been relatively free of government oversight. Singapore is becoming a popular destination for Vietnamese students because of its proximity, relatively low cost, high standards, and status as an Asian country. Tuition fees are one-third those of universities in the U.S. or the U.K.

The majority of Vietnamese students abroad study in Australia, but U.S. institutions command great respect from Vietnamese institutions and students alike. Many Vietnamese university administrators and other officials concede that most Australia-bound students—90 percent, according to a recent U.S. embassy analysis—would rather study in the United States, given the opportunity.

Vietnamese young people—full of energy, ambition, and a desire to be challenged that is not being fulfilled in their country's institutions of higher education—are intrigued by Western cultures. In the words of one Vietnamese student, they want to "do something" in a system that does not give them sufficient knowledge, skills, or freedom of action to realize their potential or, in many cases, even to find gainful employment. For them, overseas study is a means to that end.

A recent trend is the establishment of high-quality joint degree programs in cooperation with universities in Australia, Belgium, the Netherlands, the U.S., and other countries that enable students to take courses taught by both Vietnamese and foreign professors, sometimes in Vietnamese and sometimes in English. Examples include the M.B.A. program at the Hanoi School of Business, affiliated with Vietnam National University (VNU), and several graduate degree programs offered through the National Economics University (NEU). The Hanoi School of Business offers a two-year M.B.A. program, taught in English, with a curriculum that includes lectures, case studies, field studies, and team projects, as well as state-of-the-art technology and up-to-date facilities. The cost of tuition is just under $5,000, expensive but within reach of many of the sons and daughters of Vietnam's urban middle class.

Regional Differences

The prevailing view among expatriates and Vietnamese alike is that Vietnam is actually three countries, each with unique qualities and characteristics that derive from very different histories and conditions. Although these regional traits are generalizations that can be a source of amusement for some Vietnamese and foreigners, they are also useful in better understanding the differences between people. Unlike other areas, where regional differences in mentality and outlook are often attributed to climate (e.g., northern versus southern Europe), the explanations in Vietnam can be found in history.

Vietnam was first split in half during a war that lasted from 1627 to 1772. The country was reunified in the late eighteenth century and was called "Viet Nam" for the first time in 1804. It was during the French colonial era that Vietnam was divided into three parts. The northern and central regions were protectorates, while the south was administered as a colony.

Northerners are considered to be more intelligent, conservative, austere, serious, and frugal than their fellow citizens in the central and southern parts of the country. Some Vietnamese say that northerners' aloofness can, at times, border on arrogance. They are more apt to "save for a rainy day"; some speculate that this is the result of their long experience with a centralized economy and government, under which people were supposed to pretend to be very poor or risk being viewed as capitalists, a "dirty word" in those days. As many foreigners will attest, people from the north are also warm, friendly, sincere, and trustworthy. They are considered to be more hardworking and inclined to planning because of the harsh conditions under which they lived for so long.

Many of Vietnam's leaders come from the central region of the country, a poor area with few natural resources that is known for its tough conditions. Vietnamese from the central region are seen as iron-willed, courteous, unafraid to assume responsibility, and willing to go the extra mile in whatever they undertake. It is said that the difficult living conditions have helped shaped the way they think and act (e.g., the land is not fertile for agriculture, and the region is prone to natural disasters). They are known to be hardworking and are considered particularly adept at learning. Many leave their hometowns and villages for the city, where they become successful. In another common view, they are seen as less generous than the people of the north or the south, and this is considered one reason that they not only have been successful, but also have become rich.

The first Viet settlers reached the Mekong Delta in the seventeenth century. Described by Huu Ngoc as "famished peasants, peasant-soldiers, adventurers, and banished criminals," these settlers found a land of rich soil; therefore, they "did not have the hard work and chronic want that were the lot of northern farmers, plagued by the scarcity of land and the frequency of natural calamities such as floods" (1997, 260). Perhaps because their lot was easy, southerners are perceived as fun-loving, easy-going, open people who rarely think of saving for a rainy day. They are also seen as courageous and law-abiding, and as more direct—which means that their style is more compatible with that of most Westerners.

As one transplanted northerner put it, in the south, which is tropical, while the north has four seasons, "You can go to the garden, eat, go to a river or pond and fish. Life is easier. Have a beer. Sleep well." He added, tongue in cheek, "You see northerners running the south because they have guns and are smarter." Since 1975, many people have moved from the north to the south for government positions (in line with the postwar goal of placing politically loyal, "reliable" people in positions of power in the south) and, more recently, to make money. In some cases, their family and friends follow. Southern men have a reputation for drinking a lot, as anyone who has staggered off to bed after a night of socializing with southerners in Vietnam (or abroad) can confirm. They believe that money and life are for enjoying today, without worrying about tomorrow.

Many expatriates claim that it is easier to do business in the south because there are more English- and French-speaking people who are more accustomed to dealing with foreigners, and there is more of a frontier spirit. In contrast to the North, which was closed to the outside world in 1954, the South was open until unification and the end of the war in

1975. (One relevant legal distinction, as mentioned earlier, is that the North was a protectorate, while the South was a colony, which means it was more open and susceptible to influence from other countries.) As every expatriate will advise, you can set up an office in HCM City or elsewhere in the southern part of the country, but Hanoi—with all of the ministries, the parliament, the Party, the embassies—is where the real decision-making power is, and you ignore this at your own peril.

Interestingly, recent research has found that managers from the North seem to exhibit a more Western-oriented attitude toward individualism, whereas managers in the south seem to hold a more traditionally Asian collectivist position. As the authors of one study put it, the North is facing West while the South is facing East!

Male–Female Relationships

Nationally, Vietnamese women make up just over 50 percent of the workforce and are guaranteed legal rights that were denied to them during colonial times. Nevertheless, Vietnam is still very much a patriarchal society. In Confucianism, the patriarchal family is the main unit of society, in which duties and obligations are delineated as those of a family to a father, a child to a parent, a wife to a husband, and a younger brother to an older brother. This explains the pressure placed on women by their husbands and in-laws to produce male heirs. In addition, sons are still viewed as their parents' main source of support in old age. It is said that many men tell their wives *before* marriage that they want to have "a girl as lovely as you," but *after* marriage that they want only sons. In many cases, it is common for women to say that they want to give their husbands a son or, if pregnant, to say that they feel that the baby will be a son.

As one Vietnamese woman put it, many women contribute to making their daughters second-class citizens: "Instead of opposing her husband's unequal idea, she anxiously awaits the ultrasound result, completely forgetting that she has become the slave of another's thinking. The climax is 'showing off' the gender of the baby and feeling pity for the others because they are waiting to have a child who is the same 'kind' as you."

Although women were often equal partners during wartime, men now hold most of the positions of power and influence in the government, the business world, and academia. The situation is slightly different in the nonprofit sector, where some Vietnamese women are employed as country directors, not just as secretaries and other support staff. As in other societies, women who hold high-ranking positions are held to the double standard of meeting both their professional and their domestic obligations with equal success and diligence. In another example of the old coexisting and sometimes conflicting with the new, socialist ideals of equality contradict traditional Confucianist thought that subordinates girls and women to fathers, husbands, and sons. Women are responsible for family harmony, which means that wives should be passive, industrious, and obedient to their husbands and in-laws.

Referring to a situation that is not unique to Vietnam, one career-minded young Vietnamese woman wrote about how different her generation is from that of her mother and grandmother:

> You and I—we work, we have money and we are equal to men. Society respects us, praises us. The Vietnam Women's Union even has awards with seemingly attractive and honorable names like "Good official, better housewife." The more it praises, the more we manage. We try hard to make everything run smoothly: housework (cooking, cleaning, washing), company work (meetings, advertising, managing). Being busy with loads of work, have we ever stopped to ask ourselves: "Why do we have to work so hard like this?"

What's more, as Le Thi Nham Tuyet, founder of the Research Center for Gender, Family, and Environment in Development, notes, "The focus on making money has created new stresses in families, and we're seeing a rise in domestic violence, a preference for male children, and a growing inequality in access to education for girls." (Ford Foundation report, *www.fordfound.org/publications/ff_report/view_ff_report_detail.cfm?report_index=4*).

According to a 2002 United Nations Development Programme report, using data from a domestic source (the Vietnam Women's Union [VWU]), 80 percent of Vietnamese women have experienced some form of violence, including neglect, verbal abuse, beatings, and forced sex. One study found that virtually all men and the majority of women surveyed believed that it was acceptable for a man to abuse his wife. The report noted that "much of the blame is placed on the gender stereotypes which keep women and men in prescribed roles and which maintain an unequal power balance between them." The men cited alcohol or temper as contributing factors toward their violence, while women, "in the tradition of stoic Vietnamese womanhood, accept it as normal" (*http://news.bbc.co.uk/ 2/hi/asia-pacific/2349059.stm*).

The Vietnamese government's adviser on women, Tran Thi Mai Huong, stated that Vietnam must shift its approach from seeing gender inequity as a women's issue to ensuring that gender issues are discussed at all levels of society and policymaking. In December 2003, the VWU proposed that the National Assembly create a Law on Gender Equality to demonstrate Vietnam's commitment to eliminating discrimination against women.

Among women who return from an overseas study experience, there are stories of recent graduates who reenter a culture that frowns upon women who have "too much education" or are "too smart." In one instance, a woman with an M.B.A. from a prestigious U.S. university was unable to find a suitable position and ended up working abroad for an international government agency. In another case, a woman broke off her engagement with her M.A.-educated fiancé because he asked her to make a choice: either return with him to Vietnam and get married, or pursue a Ph.D. She chose the latter.

Not only is it difficult for women to find a position that matches their qualifications, but their level of education can actually make it difficult to get married. This is especially problematic in a country where women are on their way to becoming "old maids" by the time they reach their mid-twenties. (The age at which most women marry is lower in the villages, usually between eighteen and twenty; for high school dropouts, it can be as young as sixteen.) In fact, the Vietnamese have an expression that means "Girls need not study further because it would be hard to find husbands." Once the marriage clock begins ticking, pressure increases among family and friends to find a suitable partner. Introductions are made, hints dropped, encouragement offered. To compound this problem, many Vietnamese men consider younger women to be more desirable marriage partners, meaning that, for single women, the pool of eligible marriage partners shrinks dramatically with the passing of each year. (One of the sad postwar ironies was that women who had contributed to the war effort were too old to find a husband when peace finally arrived. There was also the stark realization that so many men of that generation died during the war. As a consolation prize of sorts, the government permitted them to have children out of wedlock.)

Aside from being discriminatory from a Western perspective, this view of women and education is inefficient and costly in a country that desperately needs women's knowledge, experience, and skills. Among those Vietnamese who have received advanced education and training abroad, those most likely to prosper are married, male government employees who are returning to their former place of employment. Only in rare cases do Vietnamese women, who usually live at home until marriage, have the support of their parents to fulfill their dream of a career or higher education.

Thus, many women are forced to make the emotionally wrenching decision to sacrifice their education and, possibly, their long-range career plans for a relationship, or to continue their education in the hope that they will find love with a man of equal status or with one who is not so concerned about his wife's level of education (a very progressive-minded Vietnamese, an overseas Vietnamese, or another foreigner). And, of course, there are some exceptions, Vietnamese husbands who do support their wives' quest for professional development and even overseas study.

If you are working in Vietnam, you should expect to work in a male-dominated world in which most of women will be low-level assistants and secretaries, not colleagues with major decision-making responsibility. Most of your male counterparts, however, are accustomed to foreign women in a business setting. If you are a woman, rest assured that most of your male colleagues will see you through different lenses than they would a Vietnamese woman. As with foreign men, they will generally judge you not on your gender but on how you conduct yourself, your knowledge and experience, the capability of your company or organization, and a variety of other factors having nothing to do with gender. In some cases, your gender may even make you exempt from such customs as drinking excessively during after-hours socializing, time used to strengthen and cement working relationships—an "exemption" that can have both positive and negative connotations.

Looking Ahead

What Vietnam has accomplished in a very short time borders on the miraculous. The World Bank estimates that 70 percent of all households were living in poverty in the 1980s. By 2002, that figure had dropped to 29 percent. This was accompanied by an improvement in social indicators, including decreased mortality rates for children under five.

But, as the World Bank and other international lending agencies are fond of pointing out, the Vietnamese still need opportunities that those in wealthy countries take for granted, such as the chance to work and provide for a family. To promote private-sector growth and job creation, countries like Vietnam have to improve their financial and economic management, legal systems, and physical infrastructure such as roads, power, and water.

One of Vietnam's great challenges will be to continue educational reforms so that its schools, universities, and colleges are in step with the current and projected needs of a market economy. On the economic front, Vietnam will have to create jobs for the 1.5 million young people who enter the job market every year. It is said that there is a new crisis among the youth—that they have become depoliticized, that their value system in this "market economy with socialist orientation" is based on the dollar bill (Boudarel and Nguyen 2002, 6).

Core Cultural Dimensions

The Vietnamese and Asians in general know how to
maintain a relationship. In the West you might become
friends, but you can do business without *becoming friends.*
In Asia, you must become friends before doing business.

—Vietnamese manager

Most people are friendly, and social interaction is an
important part of life. It is a kind of interdependent society
with different relationships among people.

—Vietnamese student

This chapter takes a closer look at Vietnam as a collectivist society in which the group takes precedence over the individual, communication is about more than words and literal meaning, relationships are key, and harmony is the goal of virtually every activity and interaction. A number of related aspects of Vietnamese culture—community and collectivism, indirect communication, nonverbal communication, and other cultural dimensions related to harmony—are discussed in this chapter. Then, in Chapter 6, these are applied specifically to a work setting.

Community and Collectivism

Societies such as Australia, Canada, Germany, the Netherlands, the U.K., and the U.S. all, to varying degrees, value individualism. They emphasize the importance of the individual's freedom, independence, and happiness over that of the group. Asian cultures, by contrast, place a higher value on the group and tend to see individuals in terms of their membership in and obligation to groups. The following chart (Ferraro 2002, 101) offers a general comparison of individual- and collective-oriented societies that is helpful in understanding Vietnamese culture.

Individual-Oriented Societies	*Collective-Oriented Societies*
Individuals are major units of social perception.	Groups are major units of social perception
Explain others' behavior by personal traits.	Explain others' behavior by group norms.
Success attributed to own ability.	Success attributed to help of group.
Self defined as individual entity.	Self defined in terms of group.
Know more about self than others.	Know more about others than self.
Achievement for one's own sake.	Achievement for benefit of group.
Personal goals over group goals.	In-group goal over personal goals.
Values self-assuredness.	Values modesty.
Values autonomy and independence.	Values interdependence.
Fears dependence on others.	Fears ostracism.
Casual connections to many groups.	Strong connection to a few groups.
Few obligations to others.	Many obligations to others.
Confrontation is acceptable.	Harmony is expected.
Task completion is important.	Relations are important.

Reprinted with permission from *The Cultural Dimension of International Business,* 4th ed., by Gary P. Ferraro (Upper Saddle River, NJ: Prentice Hall, 2002), p. 101.

Without understanding the differences listed here, it is obvious why uninitiated Westerners sometimes view Vietnamese humility and modesty as deceitful and see their indirectness and consensus-building efforts as mere bureaucratic red tape—"the old runaround." On other side of the same coin, Vietnamese, who often view individual assertiveness as arrogant, may see Westerners' directness as tactless and even aggressive.

Family and *que huong* ("home village"; the site of one's ancestors' graves) are high priorities for Vietnamese; these concepts, which permeate daily life and language, play a more important role in Vietnam than in most Western cultures. Vietnamese are delighted when foreign friends and colleagues ask about the health and activities of their family members or when an expat supervisor is sensitive to the importance of attending to family-related needs that may arise during business hours. In a recurring theme in our interviews with expats and Vietnamese alike, the Vietnamese often describe productive work organizations as "like a family" and less productive ones as "not like a family" (Borton 2001, 7).

In Vietnam, every person has his place within the family, the village, and the larger society. One's place determines one's duties, responsibilities, and privileges. Compared with some other Asian cultures, however, relationships are not as formalized in Vietnam; they do not constitute a vertical line of hierarchical power but, rather, a complicated web of shared stories, favors, obligations, rights, and points of accountability that form the basis for interdependence at all levels of society (Borton 2001, 4–5). For most Vietnamese, these networks of relationships are a matter of social security and even of survival.

The Vietnamese language reflects these relationships through its many pronouns for *you* and *I*. Most pronouns name family relationships on the basis of a paternal/maternal branched hierarchy that, for example, differentiates *uncle* into a half dozen words and identical twins into "older" and "younger." Pronouns change according to speakers' respective ages, sex, social status, and level of intimacy, with every pronoun establishing and reinforcing a specific relationship (Borton 2001, 5). This explains why Vietnamese will ask your age, a taboo subject in many Western societies: your answer will enable your colleague to define your relationship in his own language and cultural mindscape.

Just as every Vietnamese has her place, so every expatriate organization and individual belongs somewhere in the Vietnamese system. The government office where an organization belongs is similar to a Vietnamese older sibling, who takes care of and protects the younger. The office obtains expatriate visas, signs off on permissions, and assumes responsibility on the Vietnamese side. In trying times, this point of contact can be the project's most ardent advocate and supporter. This family analogy explains the importance of frequent and close communication as a means of "staying on the same page."

All foreign organizations and individuals belong somewhere, with the site dependent on the type of the work and the administrative level dependent on the size of the project. Foreign businesses belong to the Ministry of Planning and Investment (MPI); international NGOs to the People's Aid Coordinating Committee (PACCOM); academic institutions to the Ministry of Education and Training or Ministry of Science, Technology, and Environment (MOSTE); journalists to the Foreign Press Center (Borton 2001, 10). Vietnam is not a place for mavericks, lone wolves, or people who find it difficult to work as part of a cross-cultural team.

Indirect Communication

Like other Asian societies, Vietnam is classified as a "high-context society." This complex and important concept has been the topic of countless books and articles in the field of intercultural communication. In *Understanding Cultural Differences* (1996), Hall and Hall define a high-context communication, or message, as one in which most of the information already is in the person, while very little is in the coded, explicit, transmitted part of the message. In a low-context communication, by contrast, most of the information is in the explicit code—the words themselves.

Hall and Hall offer a concrete example by contrasting high-context Japanese, Arabs, and Mediterranean peoples with low-context U.S. Americans, Germans, Swiss, Scandinavians, and other northern Europeans. The former societies tend to be homogeneous and have extensive information networks among family, friends, colleagues, and clients; the latter tend to be more heterogeneous and to compartmentalize personal relationships, work, and many other aspects of daily life. In these low-context societies, each time people interact with others, they need detailed background information.

People in high-context societies such as Vietnam do not need or expect detailed background information about the people they're dealing with because they make a point of keeping themselves informed about everything that has to do with the important people in their lives (Hall and Hall 1996, 6–7). In this type of society, *whom* you know is as important as *what* you know. Because a high-context communication is one in which most of the information is in the person, people from high-context societies may think that those from low-context cultures talk too much (sometimes without saying a lot), while the latter complain that the former are too quiet (and therefore are probably hiding something).

The U.S. Peace Corps training manual *Culture Matters* (found online at *www.peacecorps.gov/wws/culturematters*) lists a number of characteristics and behaviors that are found in high-context cultures. These are familiar to expatriates and to Vietnamese with cross-cultural experience.

- Communication is like that between twins. (High-context people have the kind of instinctive understanding that is common with twins.)
- People are reluctant to say no. (Refusal threatens harmony, which is key in high-context cultures.)
- Use of intermediaries or third parties is common. (Third-party communication avoids direct conflict.)
- Use of understatement is frequent. (Understatement is more indirect.)
- "Yes" means only "I hear you." (Where it's difficult to say no, yes has less meaning.)
- People engage in small talk and catching up before getting down to business. (Relationships are important in high-context cultures.)
- Lukewarm tea means all is not well. (The message is often not in the words, so look for it elsewhere.)

- People are already up-to-date. (Close-knit networks are common in more collectivist, high-context cultures, so look for the message elsewhere.)
- The rank or status of the messenger is as important as the message. (The message is not only in the words; look for it in something else.)
- People tell you what they think you want to hear. (So you won't be upset.) (*www.peacecorps.gov/wws/culturematters*)

In most Western societies, people are brought up to believe that it's best to be "honest"—to tell it like it is. This view is expressed in many ways: "Yes means yes," or "What you see is what you get" (meaning that it's not necessary to read between the lines), or "Business first, chit-chat later," or "The message is more important than the messenger."

People in high-context cultures already know and understand each other very well and, therefore, have developed a more indirect style of communication that relies more on context and on nonverbal communication. Getting to the point—so highly valued in most Western societies, in which you are expected to introduce your main point and offer supporting evidence and justification—is achieved in a more circuitous fashion in Vietnam. Vietnamese may tell stories while moving slowly but surely in the direction of the main point. As both Vietnamese and savvy expats point out, they are not trying to play the stereotypical "inscrutable Oriental" or to drive you crazy—they are simply being respectful and tactful.

One Vietnamese writer illustrates indirectness with this humorous story of a mandarin's sumptuous feast. A servant waiting on guests compliments the mandarin on his robe. The servant describes how the mulberry trees were planted and how they grew and how their leaves were gathered; how the silkworms were fed and how they grew and how they spun their cocoons; how (speaking a bit faster now) the cocoons were boiled and how silken thread was gathered from the worms' cocoons and spun; how (speaking even faster) the brocade was woven with gold and silver threads and then embroidered, too; and how (speaking faster still) the robe was perfectly tailored to fit the mandarin's august and magnificent frame. Finally, the breathless servant blurts: "Sire, your robe is on fire!" (Borton 2001, 8).

Here is a more mundane but equally telling example from daily life, involving a recently married Vietnamese woman and her mother-in-law. As is the custom, she and her husband live with his parents. The young woman has a conversation with her mother-in-law about how her sister has said she will not visit on a regular basis unless the young woman and her husband have their own place. What she is saying, indirectly, is that she would prefer to live with her husband on their own when they can afford it. Her aim is to avoid at all costs offending her mother-in-law, whom she respects and with whom, in fact, she gets along. Although it is true that her sister would prefer to visit them in their own place, this is also an indirect way of expressing her own shared sentiment.

Here are some common examples of indirect communication that you will hear in Vietnam, taken from the Peace Corps workbook *Culture Matters* (*www.peacecorps.gov/wws/culturematters*). The left-hand column shows what a Vietnamese partner might say, while the right-hand column contains possible "translations": interpretations from a Western standpoint, as well as suggested responses.

Vietnamese Indirect Statement	*Correct Interpretation for Westerners*
That is a very interesting viewpoint.	I don't agree. We need to talk more about this. You're wrong. We don't like it.
This proposal deserves further consideration.	It needs work. Propose something else. I'm something of an expert on this but am too polite to say so.

Vietnamese Indirect Statement	Correct Interpretation for Westerners
I know very little about this, but . . .	What I think we should do is . . .
	We understand your proposal very well.
	We don't like it.
Do you have another one?	We will try our best.
	Don't expect much to happen.
I heard another story about that project.	I don't agree with what you said about that project.
	We don't want to talk about this now.
Can we move on to the next topic?	We need to consult with people not in the room before we can decide.

Of course, one of the purposes of conversation is to build a personal relationship, without which there can be no business relationship. Westerners, especially those with a "time is money" orientation, will quickly lose patience if they are unaware of the rationale and dynamics of an indirect style of communication. It is important to let relationships unfold naturally, without being overly anxious or forceful. Several expats explained how they speak with a Vietnamese voice by first describing how an issue is dealt with elsewhere and only then proceeding to the main point—which, with a Westerner, they would normally make first. Once they get to know you—once a foundation of trust, acceptance, and understanding is firmly in place—your Vietnamese counterparts will be open and honest and will eagerly offer advice and guidance.

Understanding "Yes, Yes"

Foreigners often assume that "Yes, yes" means agreement when, in fact, the phrase only means, "I'm listening." Some businesses and international NGOs have gone so far as to plan events, print programs, invite consultants, and even meet their guests at the airport, only to discover that their Vietnamese partners never agreed to host the events. A Westerner traveled to Vietnam for an event limited to Vietnamese. Although she had heard "Yes, yes" to her request to attend, she had never received even a verbal invitation. Her mistake was in not "listening" to what her Vietnamese colleagues were telling her and failing to determine whether or not their plans and goals were compatible at that stage of the relationship (Borton 2001, 12–13).

In Vietnam, the words for affirmation during negotiations are "agree" or "consent," whether in Vietnamese or translated into another language. When Vietnamese colleagues say, "Yes, yes," check to confirm the actual meaning and determine if they have any doubts or suggestions—don't assume they're saying, "Yes, I agree."

Listening for "No"

Like other Asians, Vietnamese rarely say no. A refusal causes a loss of face, and, as the Vietnamese expression goes, "Better to die than to lose face." Of course, there are ways of communicating disagreement and negative decisions, but Westerners often misunderstand and misinterpret these messages. Vietnamese usually say "No" indirectly through expressions like these: "It's complicated." "It's a little difficult." "It's not the right time." "There's a problem." Upon hearing one of these phrases, most Westerners are inclined to want to solve the "problem" rather than addressing the real concerns, setting the issue aside, or finding another way to reach agreement. Westerners also should look for nonverbal indications that "No" is the answer, including the use of silence. Lady Borton offers this advice to foreigners wondering how to respond to this situation:

> Try something like, "If anything is complicated or difficult, if this isn't the right time, or if there's a problem, just let me know. We'll stop, or change directions, or wait." These techniques are also useful as responses to a Vietnamese "No," since they open the way

for small steps towards a mutually acceptable solution. This approach may seem perplexing to those beset by project plans, deadlines, and a bottom line. However, in the yin and yang of Vietnamese culture, yielding control creates trust and access. (2001, 14)

Responses like these give the Vietnamese flexibility and room to maneuver. The wording is also a recognition that most issues are not black and white but, rather, play out in a gray area.

Nonverbal Communication

What follows is a summary of nonverbal behaviors and their meanings in Vietnamese culture.

Nonverbal Behavior	*Meaning in Vietnamese Culture*
Nodding	Greeting; affirmative reply; agreement
Shaking one's head	Negative reply; disagreement
Bowing	Greeting; great respect
Touching a child's head	Not appreciated, but not offensive
Avoiding eye contact	Showing respect to people senior in age or status or of the opposite sex
Winking	Not acceptable, especially when directed at people of the opposite sex
Frowning	Frustration, anger, or worry
Pouting	Disdain
Smiling	Agreement; embarrassment; disbelief; mild disagreement; appreciation; apology

Nonverbal Behavior	*Meaning in Vietnamese Culture*
Shaking hands	Friendly greeting between men (but not the elderly)
	Not customary between women or between a man and a woman; acceptable between a Vietnamese woman and non-Vietnamese man
Palm of right hand out, fingers moving up and down several times	"Come here." Not used with people senior in age or status.
Holding hands with or putting an arm over the shoulder or a person of the same sex	Friendly gesture with no sexual connotation
Holding hands with or putting an arm over the shoulder of a person of the opposite sex	Not usually done in public
Crossing arms	Sign of respect
Placing one or both hands in the pockets or the hips while talking	Arrogance; lack of respect
Patting a person's back, especially someone senior in age or status	Disrespectful
Pointing to other people while talking	Disrespectful, threatening
Putting one's feet on a table or sitting on a desk while talking	Rude

When a Smile Is Not a Smile

The Asian smile has been aptly described as the "regional mask" worn to disguise the degree and nature of a problem, or even the fact that one exists. In contrast to the West, where a smile usually indicates happiness or amusement, in Vietnam it can mask embarrassment, anger, fear, anxiety, or disagreement. In *Understanding Vietnam,* Neil Jamieson tells the story of a brief encounter between an American manager and one of his Vietnamese employees that involved a cross-cultural misunderstanding resulting from a smile.

> I once saw an American point out to a Vietnamese employee that he had made a rather serious error. The American explained the situation earnestly and with great patience. The Vietnamese listened intently. When the American finished, the Vietnamese grinned from ear to ear and did not say a word. For a moment the American stared at him in amazement, then abruptly lost his temper. "Look at that son-of-a-bitch! He thinks it's funny!" The smile had indicated embarrassment; the silence, agreement and acceptance of fault. The employee had understood the explanation, accepted responsibility for the problem, and would probably have corrected the deficiency at the earliest possible moment. But the American had expected some verbal response: an explanation, a denial, an apology, or even an argument. He interpreted the silence as disinterest and the smile as impertinence. (1995, 75–76)

Thus, contrary to the saying that the whole world smiles in the same language, the Vietnamese smile can convey a number of meanings and may conceal a variety of emotions, as mentioned earlier in this section.

As Chapter 6 will point out, it is unacceptable to show anger or other strong emotions in Vietnam. To do so is not only embarrassing but also can result in a loss of face. Whereas most Westerners will frown or scowl when angry or irritated, Vietnamese will smile. Vietnamese are also unlikely to tell you directly that they do not understand something you have said. Instead, they will probably smile when they do not understand something. When foreigners see two Vietnamese riding motorbikes that nearly collide, they are puzzled when the bikers drive off smiling. These smiles are not a sign of happiness; rather, they reflect nervousness, an unspoken apology, or a way of saying, "Take it easy. It's no big deal." A smile is also a form of nonverbal communication that can mean "Thank you" or "Yes, I appreciate or acknowledge what you've done."

As with other intercultural skills, you will soon learn to distinguish between those smiles that denote happiness and those that are masking other emotions. Be sure to look for other clues to what is really going on. The answers lie in the context and in other aspects of nonverbal communication.

Other Cultural Dimensions Related to Harmony

Once you understand the importance of harmony as a centerpiece of Vietnamese interaction, other aspects of Vietnamese culture come into focus as ways of achieving that goal. These are some of the most important.

The Concept of Face

"Face" refers to what others think or say about you. As in other Asian cultures, saving face is highly valued by the Vietnamese as a way of maintaining respect and harmony in interpersonal relations. This explains why the Vietnamese prepare very carefully what to say or to do in order not to hurt others' feelings. The emphasis on face also means that Vietnamese will try to perform a task flawlessly. If you have a suggestion, advice, or criticism for your Vietnamese colleague or partner, it is best to use an indirect approach or even humor. Avoid a condescending attitude. It's better to propose a number of possible solutions rather than to focus on a problem. Saving face as a part of maintaining harmony is essential in Vietnam. The following cross-cultural dialogue illustrates the dangers of criticizing someone directly—in this case, an employee in a public setting.

Mr. Hansen: I appreciate how hard all of you have been working in recent weeks. This is a busy time for all of us. Mr. Luong, I was hoping you would have finished that report yesterday. Can you get it to me by tomorrow morning?

Mr. Luong: Yes, I'm very sorry it is late.

Mr. Hansen: It's OK. You're usually very efficient and good in meeting important deadlines.

Mr. Luong: *(looking down; voice lower)* I apologize. I will give it to you as soon as I can.

Mr. Hansen: Thank you. Now, let's talk about our colleagues from the home office who will be visiting us next week.

The damage has already been done with Mr. Hansen's criticism of Mr. Luong in front of the other staff. If you do have to reprimand your local staff, it is best to speak with the offending individual privately. Avoid talking about an individual's mistakes or inadequacies in front of other local staff. To do so will poison your relationship not only with the individual in question but also with the entire staff. The same principle applies to praise: do not reward employees by singling them out for praise, unless you do so in private.

Respect

Vietnamese pronouns may be variable, but the basic premise is always respect. Vietnamese strive to increase the respect given to the addressee while diminishing the respect applied to oneself; in Vietnamese, this can be done by choosing a high-status variant of *you* and a lower-status version of *I*. Because the English language has no equivalent, Westerners will need to compensate by using gracious phrases such as "If it's all right with you, I'd like to suggest an idea. . . ." or "Please allow me to suggest . . ."

Gestures are also important. The primary gesture of respect is a gentle bow. On first meeting, Vietnamese shake hands and usually look down or to the side, indicating respect for the other person. The handshake is gentle, also indicating respect. Westerners often misinterpret these gestures as signs of weakness, while Vietnamese can easily view the Westerner's strong handshake and direct eye contact as arrogance (Borton 2001, 5–6).

Sense of Time

To establish consensus and preserve harmony, the Vietnamese have a tendency to discuss issues in great detail, analyzing a problem from every conceivable angle until a solution is found. This includes consultation at every stage of the process. So although punctuality for an appointment or meeting is valued, the Vietnamese take a more liberal view of time when it comes to reaching agreement and consummating a deal. This runs counter to the predominantly Western view that you shouldn't put off until tomorrow what you can do today. A Vietnamese manager who frequently travels abroad and has worked with people from all over the world states it succinctly: "In Vietnam there are two approaches to efficiency, defined as doing things right, and effectiveness, defined as doing the right things. Doing the right thing is the most important." Sometimes, "doing the right thing" can be time-consuming (Borton 2001).

Comprehensive Consultation

Comprehensive consultation is a way to achieve consensus, which, in turn, ensures harmony. In Vietnamese this is known as *xin phep,* meaning "Allow me . . . ," "Permit me . . . ," or "Be kind enough to listen to me. . . ." For Westerners, comprehensive consultation implies a loss of influence, yet *xin phep* has little to do with the yes and no of control. For a Vietnamese, *xin phep* shows respect and an acknowledgment of the appropriate relationship; it invites group input, builds consensus, and develops support to ensure that a project runs smoothly. To Westerners, a consensus culture often seems tedious and long-winded, an unwelcome reminder that the devil really is in the details. Failure to follow the rules and ethos of comprehensive consultation will likely result in lost productivity and burned bridges.

One way to build consensus is to use phrases with tentative wording such as "If you agree, we thought we might . . ." This provides an opening to describe a project's central idea and rationale, adding more detail than is usual in the West. In Vietnam, it is best not to take proposed steps until everyone is comfortable. Effective expatriates *xin phep* with Vietnamese colleagues about anything and everything that affects those colleagues" (Borton 2001, 11–12). Building trust through consultation about seemingly insignificant details will make quick decisions possible for larger projects in the future.

The culture of foreign organizations seems as alien to Vietnamese staff as Vietnamese culture does to the newly arrived expatriate. As a senior Vietnamese staff person at one UN agency put it, "We Vietnamese look to expatriate managers to set standards. We know we can learn, but micro-managers soon lose our respect. When faced with managers who won't listen, we stop taking initiative. Soon we stop offering essential advice. Often the expatriate begins to fail, but doesn't even know it" (Borton 2001, 17–18). This sentiment is echoed in Chapter 7, "How the Vietnamese See Westerners."

Vietnamese Cultural Categories

One of the most effective ways to understand another culture is to compare and contrast fundamental values and attitudes of one's own culture with those of the host culture. This concluding section focuses on a wide range of attitudes, views, and values from a Vietnamese perspective.

It is interesting to note that, because Vietnam is changing so quickly, some attitudes now resemble those of the West, especially those that have been influenced by the "market economy with a socialist orientation" and by Vietnam's contact with the rest of the world over the past ten years. Generational differences also exist. The views expressed here are not based on a scientific sampling but, rather, reflect common strands found in surveys with Vietnamese.

Attitude toward Age

In Vietnam, age is still highly valued. The prevailing view is that older people deserve respect because of their experience, knowledge, and wisdom. This attitude is changing somewhat: the young are seen as more dynamic, with an ability to learn faster, two important qualities in the world of work. As a result of the country's economic reforms, many urban Vietnamese are becoming more like Westerners in some respects, with a greater emphasis on achievement and results. Nevertheless, *how* you do things remains more important than the results.

Concept of Fate and Destiny

Vietnamese parents influence the way children think about who and what they can become. Without money, power, and connections, you can't simply be whatever you want to be. The Vietnamese believe that each -person has a fate or destiny that is beyond her control. If one is not born into a doctor's family, for example, chances are that one will have to give up the dream of becoming a doctor. But there is a caveat: like other traditional values, parental influence is weakening somewhat, with a shift toward the belief that individuals are responsible for their own future.

View of Human Nature

Vietnamese people are more alert and reserved than are Westerners when dealing with strangers. They are likely to hold the view that even those who appear to be your friends today may turn against you tomorrow, so you should not trust other people but only yourself, or those who have been introduced by a friend or family member. The Vietnamese are not open to strangers and take awhile to accept them. They also believe that if someone commits an evil act, it is in part because of the surrounding environment. A central Buddhist belief shared by most Vietnamese is that human beings are naturally good but become bad when they yield to temptation.

Attitude toward Change and Risk

Change means risk and thus is not always readily accepted, although it is generally acknowledged that change is necessary for development. People in Vietnam are still adjusting to the new style of working and thinking brought about by the economic reforms. For example, many would rather take a stable job in a state agency with a lower income and moonlight to earn extra money than accept a job with higher pay for a shorter period of time.

Young people, especially those who live in the cities, have a more positive view of change and are more likely to take risks than are the older generations and those who live in the countryside, for whom tradition is still very strong. One view is that taking risks is a way to test one's ability to shape or change one's fate.

Concept of Suffering and Misfortune

According to one Buddhist saying, "Life means suffering." For historical and geographical reasons, Vietnamese are accustomed to hardship, although most young people try to study and work hard to improve their situation in life. It is common to cheer up a friend who is depressed by pointing out that if she is depressed, it is probably not because of anything she can control, but because of fate or the actions of others. Many Vietnamese believe that they don't control their lives, that if they if were bad in a previous life, they will suffer for that behavior in this life. So a person who is unhappy, depressed, or unlucky blames his fate and tends to accept it rather than trying to do something to change it.

Source of Self-Esteem/Self-Worth

In Vietnam, self-esteem comes from family tradition. People follow the example of their grandparents and their parents, and a child who achieves more than his parents is the pride of the family. In recent years, however, the idea of creating your own worth has come to be more valued than in the past.

Concept of Equality

There is no expectation of perfect equality in this imperfect world. Vietnamese people are treated in different ways based on their birth, power, fame, wealth, and age. Those born into more favorable conditions will have more life chances and be given more respect. Older people tend to be more conservative and to believe that they are better because they have more experience. As a result of recent reforms, however, issues of equality, especially as they relate to gender, are being more widely discussed.

Attitude toward Formality

Formality—an indication of who one is in the society and in relation to other people—is still very common in Vietnam, especially among older people and in the public sector. This is reflected in the language, which uses a variety of pronouns that vary depending on age and status. In any setting, the use of titles is essential.

Degree of Realism

The Vietnamese tend to be prepared for bad things that may happen. Since they can't predict what is going to happen, things may get either worse or better, so they should be ready to appreciate whatever the outcome is. If the situation improves, they will be happy; if it gets worse, they won't be shocked because they'll be prepared. ("Prepare for the worst, hope for the best.") The younger generation is more optimistic in this respect.

Attitude toward Action

In the traditional Vietnamese view, when people say something, they are expected to do what they say; otherwise, they are liars and are not to be trusted. Today, however, Vietnam is moving closer to a more pragmatic view of the connection between what one says and what one does.

View of the Natural World

Nature has endowed Vietnam with abundant natural resources. In the traditional view, human beings can't control nature but must know how to live with it. At the same time, though, they should try to find ways to make full use of the treasures that nature makes available to them.

Working with the Vietnamese

Things in Vietnam, particularly with the government, are not just that way because it is communist. Dismissing them as such means you won't understand a lot about Vietnamese life.

—Expatriate

This chapter offers information about working with the Vietnamese, including the bases for a successful working relationship, the proper mindset, relationship building, preparation for and conduct during your first business appointment, negotiating, socializing and gift giving, contracts, and, finally, a list of basic principles for working in Vietnam. As in Chapter 5, we include some cross-cultural dialogues that illustrate important cultural points.

Prerequisites for a Successful Working Relationship

There are several elements that form the basis of a productive and enduring working relationship with your Vietnamese partner. First, don't view yourself as superior because you happen to come from a wealthier and more "developed" country. Humility and cooperation will take you a lot farther then a desire to "run the show" or "save" Vietnam. Second, realize that the best way to develop contacts is through third-party introduction, known as sponsorship. This is an effective and usually reliable means of tapping into a network for the purpose of doing business.

Equal Partnership

The existence of cultural differences that can cause misjudgments creates the need for alertness to possible misinterpretation in a variety of areas. Expatriates who come to Vietnam thinking they have all the answers, expertise, and resources inadvertently create self-defeating scenarios by placing their Vietnamese partners in an inferior role. Demanding immediate results without adapting to the Vietnamese way and speaking with a Vietnamese "voice" can create an untenable situation.

Vietnam's poverty and its cultural style of humility often lead foreigners to underestimate the educational level, ability, and talent of the Vietnamese. Successful expatriates are those who think of themselves as equal partners with their Vietnamese colleagues and behave with grace and modesty. This is as much a matter of style and attitude—*how* they communicate—as of content—*what* they communicate. Successful expatriates will learn about the Vietnamese system. They will embrace mutual respect and friendship over paternalism. They will listen and try to view the world from their Vietnamese colleagues' perspective. By contrast, those who lecture and try to impose their ideas and agenda will usually have difficulty securing cooperation.

An experienced Australian NGO leader once entertained (and sobered) a meeting of expatriate international NGO representatives with this description:

> We Westerners scream and yell and jump up and down in one spot until we make a hole in the dirt. We keep jumping up and down in that same spot until finally the hole swallows us. But when our Vietnamese colleagues face a difficulty, they drink tea or coffee or beer as friends and work the problem out informally. (Borton 2001, 9)

Introduction and Sponsorship

Work relationships in Vietnam, as in many countries, begin through introduction, but introduction in Vietnam is more like *sponsorship,* a concept that applies both to individuals and to organizations. During the First and Second Indochina Wars with France and the U.S., small secret groups within a citizens' resistance web depended on linked sponsorships. In that setting, a mistake in introduction could be a matter of life and death. Introduction was crucial, with the introducer assuming responsibility for the introduced person's actions.

This mentality is alive and well in the Vietnam of the early twenty-first century. As Lady Borton advises in *To Be Sure . . . Work Practices in Vietnam,* "The sponsor guides the newcomer and maintains peripheral involvement and ultimate responsibility. Everything must be transparent and open in order to build trust. Careful introductions can prevent mistakes and save years of trust building. Usually, sponsorship includes preliminary conversations without the newcomer present." The sponsor needs to understand the values and goals of the introduced individual or organization. This is one reason to keep your sponsor informed of your plans, activities, and outcomes (Borton 2001, 10).

Because "most of the information is already in the person" in a high-context society such as Vietnam, each person is tapped into a different network. For this reason, it is important to have a single point of entry or "sponsor." As Vietnamese managers advise, do not try to work directly with any organization at the local level without first consulting with its headquarters. The following cross-cultural dialogue is an example of how you can expect your Vietnamese potential partner to react if you suggest consultation with people who are part of a different network or organization.

> Ms. Jennings: I'm really excited about our project. In fact, I've thought about asking another Vietnamese colleague, Mr. Loi, to join us.
> Ms. Ngoc: Yes, he's a nice man. And his company has a good reputation.

Ms. Jennings: Well, I'm sure we can sit down together and iron out any problems. He is very knowledgeable and has lots of good contacts.

Ms. Ngoc: (Nods and smiles politely.)

Ms. Jennings is clearly unaware that Ms. Ngoc can draw on her own resources and that she is uncomfortable with Ms. Jennings's suggestion. Expatriates and Vietnamese agree that foreigners who develop several sponsors for the same project only create confusion. Developing more than one sponsor is likely to lead to reduced productivity resulting from either overlap or inertia (as one sponsor waits for the other to take action) (Borton 2001, 11).

Your Mindset

Business in Vietnam is more formal and indirect than in, say, Germany, but it is less formal and more direct than in Japan. In other words, the Vietnamese code of behavior is more relaxed than in other Asian societies, where the development and maintenance of interpersonal relationships tends to be formulaic.

It is a good idea to expect the wheels to turn more slowly in Vietnam than in your country, in either the public or the private sector. Come to Vietnam with an abundance of patience and perseverance. The most important form of contact is the business meeting—and chances are that there will be a series of meetings scheduled before any business is conducted. But also build plenty of time into your schedule for additional appointments, social events, and whatever else materializes on the spur of the moment.

What initially appears to be unproductive "down time" may quickly fill up with professionally and personally rewarding meetings and other appointments that are mysteriously arranged at the last minute. Be prepared for a much higher degree of spontaneity and serendipity than you are accustomed to in your home environment. In short, be flexible and always expect the unexpected. This applies equally to the telecommunications system, the transportation infrastructure, and interpersonal relationships.

Relationship Building

In Vietnam, as in other countries in Asia and beyond, success in business is based not only on *what* you know—what you and your company or organization bring to the table in terms of knowledge, capability, and value—but also on *whom* you know. Get to know your sponsor and potential partners on a personal level. Show interest and, where appropriate, subtly demonstrate your knowledge about Vietnam, while avoiding sensitive topics such as politics or sex.

On the basis of interviews with Vietnamese businesspeople and expatriates, as well as personal experience, it is clear that some nationalities have a slight advantage over others in terms of connecting effectively with their Vietnamese counterparts. The French, for example, are generally viewed as being more adroit at nurturing relationships than, say, Danes, Germans, or U.S. Americans, who have a reputation for wanting to make money fast, for being more aggressive, and for tending to view relationships in more legalistic terms. The French and Vietnamese governments have some similarities in that both are centralized, and there is a pronounced French influence in Vietnam based on a hundred years of colonial rule. The French language incorporates many Vietnamese expressions, and vice versa. Moreover, both countries are sandwiched, geographically, between very different cultures. At the heart of the French advantage, however, is the emphasis that the French place on relationship building as a precursor to doing business.

When you go to Vietnam, be sure to leave your "time is money" mentality at home. In Vietnam, it is the relationship that precedes all else, including the bottom line. Naturally, the only way to develop a relationship with someone is to spend a lot of time with that person—eating, drinking, talking (but, in most cases, not talking about business during a meal), getting to know each other. As in other Asian societies, the Vietnamese will not do business with someone they do not know and trust.

Think of time spent having another beer or cup of tea at the end of the meal as something productive in itself, rather than as down time between substantive, productive discussions. This is the time during which your Vietnamese partner will take your measure to see where your values and intentions lie.

This was a common thread in the interviews conducted for this book: the importance of not trying to move too fast, of maintaining a good sense of where you are in the relationship with your Vietnamese colleague. What many Westerners may be inclined to view as a waste of time they should actually see as an investment in the future.

From a Vietnamese perspective, task-oriented Westerners can be perceived as inhuman, even brutal. The Western style is to focus on problems, which are, by their very nature, negative. What Westerners are lacking, from a Vietnamese point of view, is the human element. In a consensus-oriented, community culture like that of Vietnam, human beings and relationships come first, work second. Both you and your company or organization will have to readjust your priorities and style to a culture in which there are fewer time pressures and more time is required to reach consensus.

If you take the time to build up a good relationship and the mutual trust that flows from it, everything becomes possible and work can proceed at a surprisingly rapid pace. Although one of common complaints among foreigners, especially those new to the scene, is the sluggishness of the system, in fact— if all of the *t*'s have been crossed and the *i*'s dotted— the Vietnamese can move extremely fast, sometimes when you least expect it.

If you don't have this basis of trust, however, you may find that things slip through the cracks, take longer than they ought to, or are overlooked, that roadblocks are suddenly erected, that nothing quite works as it should. Think of relationship building as a kind of courtship. Find a partner whom you trust and whose values you share. Obviously, the only way to do that is by spending time together. If you identify and agree on common goals early in the relationship, so that both sides are able to measure success as well as possible failure, doing business in Vietnam can be mutually rewarding. Like marriages, successful business relationships prosper and last only if the partnership is stronger and more attractive than other possibilities.

One expat used as an example the ease with which demanding and difficult projects can be carried out because of the amount of time she has spent with her Vietnamese colleagues traveling together, eating together, overcoming problems and resolving conflicts together, acquiring a set of shared experiences—all of which makes them a family. As we have seen, the family is by far the most important unit in Vietnamese society. It evokes images of cooperation, trust, and solidarity. What can emerge from such a relationship is a kind of joint vision that allows for shared decision making about the best division of labor: who can do what the best, who knows whom, who is involved in what. This requires the participants to submerge their egos and work as a team toward common goals, an exceedingly difficult task for many Westerners, who tend to be overly concerned with getting individual recognition and credit for their contributions.

Eventually, once you have established trust with your partner, he will let you know if you are misunderstanding something or are heading in the wrong direction. Be sure to take the time to listen carefully and patiently, and ask for clarification when needed. One expat uses the image of a flooded street as a metaphor for what can happen when you don't take the time to listen. During the rainy season, some streets in Hanoi flood after an especially torrential downpour. On one particular street, people will take the manhole covers off and put sticks in them so that the water can go down more easily. If, as a foreigner, you are warned about the opening but don't listen and end up falling in, then it's your problem. At that point, in a business relationship, the Vietnamese inclination is to be gracious, take the paycheck, and go home. Another door has slammed shut.

Some Westerners have a tendency to compartmentalize work and other areas of life. Colleagues and coworkers often get to know one another by hanging out during breaks, going to lunch occasionally, and participating in other work-related activities. In most Western cultures, business lunches mean exactly that: a fixed amount of time set aside to discuss specific business matters between sips of a drink and forkfuls of food. Vietnamese, by contrast, generally do not do any work at meals unless the meal is labeled a "working lunch." Meals are viewed as a chance for colleagues to relax, tell stories, and socialize.

With enough experience, you may actually learn to enjoy this more humane and less mechanistic way of doing business. This is part of becoming bicultural—with knowledge, practice, and a period of trial and error, you begin to internalize the code of conduct of the culture in which you are working. As one old Vietnam hand put it, "Slow down, stop being a Type A personality. You will find it refreshing and enjoyable once you get used to it."

Another piece of advice that bears repeating is to be low-key. As many respondents explained, you should be subtle about the contribution that you can make, present it as an opportunity, and discuss schedule constraints. Although Vietnam is a consensus-driven society, there is a lot of room for individual initiative. "The best organizers are not sitting up on the platform," one Vietnamese respondent pointed out. "They are working on the edges. Nobody on the outside can figure out who they are. Usually, the person you want to see is the vice director, not the director, president, or chairman of the board."

Well-intentioned and motivated U.S. Americans are often guilty of coming to Vietnam with an attitude of cultural superiority, a missionary spirit that runs counter to the Vietnamese concepts of modesty, humility, and harmony (see Chapter 7 for more on this point, which was made repeatedly by Vietnamese respondents). In one case, a U.S. Fulbrighter actually tried to "run" the university to which he was assigned by interfering with the selection process for a new department chair. Many expatriates, including this Fulbrighter, act in a way that they would not behave in their own country.

All societies have both written and unwritten rules to live by. Some foreigners leave the rules of their own cultures at home but fail to adopt those of Vietnam. One expat volunteered the notion that if you just live by your own rules, you would do quite well in Vietnam. The clueless academic described above wondered why his host university had no intention of renewing his appointment for another year. Stories abound of major cultural faux pas committed by Westerners. On the bright side, however, once you have established a good relationship, with a high level of trust and complementary objectives, your ideas will begin to be taken seriously.

If you sense that there is a lack of interest on the part of your Vietnamese partner in working together, the time for a separation or divorce may be at hand. In that case, you should find a diplomatic way to let your partner ease out of the relationship without confrontation, open disagreement, or bitterness. You can speculate on the real reasons behind his change of heart, but you will probably never know for certain what happened. For example, one foreigner told a Vietnamese colleague whose interest had waned, "If you do not have enough time to work on this project, I completely understand. I know that you are very busy with your research and administrative duties. If that is the case, I know that there will be other projects we can work on together in the future at a more mutually convenient time." In this way she was able to communicate her respect and understanding, while not burning bridges and ruling out future cooperation.

The Initial Business Appointment

This section deals with such basics as scheduling an initial appointment, preparation, dress, essential protocols and customs, and tips on how the appointment will probably progress.

Scheduling the First Appointment

The first step in arranging an appointment, as discussed earlier, is to find the right individual or company to introduce you—to serve as your sponsor. Finding a suitable match of a partner organization or company at the very beginning is the way to avoid frustration and inefficiency. If you are completely new to the business scene in Vietnam, good sources of information include foreign companies, embassies, and Vietnamese and foreign chambers of commerce. Once you have identified a potential partner, you should have your sponsor arrange the appointment or, if you have no sponsor, obtain a letter of introduction from a mutual friend or acquaintance if possible. Networking with Vietnamese and foreign officials as well as businesspeople can help you make the connection, as can consultants and law firms.

If you are forced to set up an appointment without an introduction, don't just call and ask for the appointment. The best method is to send a letter requesting an appointment. Be sure to include some information about your company. Then, approximately one week later, follow up with a phone call. Your potential partner may well ask you to send another letter. At this point, however, if you mention that you have already sent a letter, he or she will be more likely to set up an initial appointment.

Even with a sponsor or an introduction, you should expect to spend a number of visits with your potential partner, getting acquainted, before attempting to get down to serious business. Always remember that an appointment spent discussing generalities and introducing yourself is time well spent and should result in the Vietnamese counterpart's increased confidence in you.

In Vietnam, appointments are usually confirmed at most one week beforehand. With high-ranking officials, the appointment may be confirmed only one or two days ahead of time and sometimes on even shorter notice. Although this makes it difficult for you to plan your trip, it is a reality in Vietnam. Generally, the better your (or your sponsor's) relationship is with the Vietnamese party, the easier it will be to secure a time.

Preparation

As in any business situation, the more you know about your prospective partner, the greater your chances of success. Nowhere is the adage that "information is power" more relevant than in Vietnam. In addition to official sources of information, the Internet is increasingly important. In the age of cell phones, which are ubiquitous, news—both positive and negative—travels with lightning speed. Word-of-mouth information can be crucial in learning about your partner's intentions, track record, integrity, credentials, and reputation. It is therefore vital to have a reliable sponsor who is either connected to the network of information or can tap into it in an indirect manner in order to be your local "eyes and ears."

As you travel to Vietnam more frequently and begin to develop your own network, this task will become much easier. When in doubt, ask a trusted Vietnamese colleague or friend about a particular individual or company. Chances are good that he or she will ask around, make a few phone calls, and get back to you with valuable information that will save you time—and possibly money as well.

One foreign educator once made the mistake of not inquiring into the reputation and trustworthiness of a Vietnamese colleague with whom he wanted to develop an academic program. He (falsely) assumed that this Vietnamese colleague was reliable because he knew someone who had worked for the man. But after several meetings, drinks, and dinners, the educator realized that his Vietnamese host was more interested in tapping into his knowledge of private higher education in the U.S. or in conducting personal or family business than in working cooperatively on a mutually beneficial program. At this point, with the assistance of another Vietnamese associate, the educator gracefully extricated myself from this budding but unproductive and pointless relationship. When he asked his Vietnamese friend more directly about the individual in question, she said she would have told him about the Vietnamese colleague's less-than-sterling reputation—had he only asked.

Dress

For men, appropriate business attire consists of a short-sleeved shirt with a tie and, on occasion (especially in Hanoi in the winter), a suit. Women may wear a pantsuit or a skirt that is cut at or below the knee. Summers in Hanoi are oppressively hot and humid, and southern Vietnam is tropical year-round, making Western business suits impractical in most situations. As is true elsewhere in Southeast Asia, business dress tends to be informal, especially when compared with the U.S. or Europe. Keep in mind that southerners tend to dress more stylishly than those in the north. For casual dress, men should wear only long pants; the only men you will see wearing shorts are tourists.

Forms of Address

In Vietnam, you should address people by their title and first name (in Vietnamese word order, this is the name that is written last) rather than their family name (which is written first). For example, if your host's name is Pham Hong Van, you would address her as Ms. Van, while Nguyen Vu Cuong would be known as Mr. Cuong. Don't be surprised if your Vietnamese colleagues, in similar fashion, address you as Mr./Ms. and your first name. Under no circumstances should a first name be used without the proper title. Some Vietnamese who are Australian- or American-educated may move fairly quickly from the use of titles to a first-name basis. Follow their lead, but don't take the initiative in using first names.

If possible, engage the services of a qualified tutor in the months leading up to your trip, and take the time and effort to learn some basic conversational Vietnamese that will allow you to greet your prospective partner and perhaps make a little small talk in their language. This will depend on your language-learning aptitude and level of comfort with the language. Of course, as in any culture, being able to speak the local or national language proficiently is ideal, but, as noted earlier, this is not always a realistic goal, especially in the case of Vietnam. As one Westerner put it, "Speaking Vietnamese made all the difference in developing relationships. Being able to make jokes in Vietnamese creates an immediate warm feeling between you and any group."

Punctuality

Punctuality is one convention that Vietnam and Western countries share. It is imperative that you show respect by arriving on time for your meeting; otherwise, you risk offending your host and getting off to a less-than-desirable start. Given the dense population and heavy traffic of Vietnam's major cities—and for your own peace of mind—allow yourself extra time to arrive for an appointment, even if you end up waiting in a car or sitting in a nearby café.

Introductions and Exchange of Business Cards

Business appointments usually begin with introductions and handshakes between men. Only shake a woman's hand if she extends hers first; this is more likely to be the case for women who have traveled, studied, or worked abroad, or have worked for many years with Westerners in Vietnam. As noted earlier, your handshake should be gentle; a strong handshake—de rigueur in the U.S. and many other countries—is perceived as arrogant in Vietnam. Using both hands is a special sign of respect and friendship and therefore is not appropriate for initial meetings.

Next comes the exchange of business cards. In typically Asian fashion, you should accept your host's card with care and study it for a moment, then place it respectfully on the table in front of you. Do not set it aside or put it in your pocket. You should give and receive business cards and other items with both hands as a sign of politeness and respect. Business cards are significant in that they tell your colleagues not only who you are but something about the organization with which you are affiliated and your position within that organization. *You will be judged, in part, on the basis of this information and the manner in which it is presented.*

For the benefit of your Vietnamese counterpart, have your business card and any other materials you bring with you translated into Vietnamese. (It is relatively easy and inexpensive to have cards printed in Vietnam.) This guarantees that your host and others in the organization who may not have a good command of English will understand who you are, what your company or organization does, and what business it proposes to undertake.

Most likely, you will be offered something to drink, such as tea or bottled water, and perhaps fruit or something else to eat. It is polite to drink some (not all) of the beverage and to eat some of whatever is offered. A man may also be offered a cigarette, which he may politely decline if he wishes.

Use of Interpreters

If you are using an interpreter, be sure to look at your host while he is speaking, as well as while the interpreter is translating what was just said. If you have not worked with an interpreter before, keep in mind that you should speak slowly and avoid slang or other colloquialisms. For the benefit of your interpreter, limit your replies to a couple of sentences at a time; this is a good way to ensure more efficient communication and avoid misunderstandings. In *The Cultural Dimension of International Business* (2002), Gary Ferraro, a U.S. professor of cultural anthropology and an intercultural trainer, advises you to establish "cordial relations" with the interpreter well in advance of your meeting so that she can understand your expectations and goals in order to best represent your interests.

After the Preliminaries

Appointments with Vietnamese colleagues are generally relaxing and enjoyable affairs as long as you are familiar with some of the key cultural differences described in this book. Appointments generally last about an hour, although there are many exceptions to this rule. After introductions state the reasons for your visit and the agenda. For the first appointment, your Vietnamese counterpart will normally begin with an introduction to his organization or company, including its history, mission statement, business lines, production capacity, export revenue, and major markets. Do not interrupt this introduction. Instead, take notes while remaining attentive, and then, after the introduction has been brought to a close, ask questions. After that, you will also want to spend some time introducing yourself and your organization or firm.

Because humility and modesty are prized qualities in Vietnam, as in other Asian countries, do not trumpet your own achievements or those of your organization. It is not that Vietnamese are not proud of their accomplishments, individual or collective, but they are likely to describe them in a more modest and inclusive fashion. Use the pronoun *I* sparingly.

As the appointment progresses, the discussion will become more detailed until each party has an understanding of what the other side can offer and how it can benefit from a possible relationship or deal. The first appointment is usually the most formal and may not even get past the introduction stage.

During this first appointment, don't rush to a discussion of the issues you came to speak about. Remember, you will probably have only an hour. If things go well, put off your agenda for later appointments. In the course of the appointment, you should expect occasional minor interruptions such a phone call or an assistant looking in to confer about something. This is normal and should not be construed as signaling boredom or a lack of interest. The following vignette illustrates how a "time is money" orientation regarding interruptions does not work in a Vietnamese context.

Mr. Smithson: It's nice to see you again. It's been a long time.

Mr. Le: Yes, welcome back to Hanoi. I look forward to working with you again.

Mr. Smithson: So let me tell you more about the project idea I mentioned to you in an e-mail a few weeks ago.

Mr. Le: (*Phone rings.*) Please excuse me for a moment.

Mr. Smithson: (*Looks at his watch.*)

Mr. Le: Yes, I remember receiving your e-mail some time ago. (*Assistant steps into the office to consult with Mr. Le.*)

Mr. Smithson: (*A look of irritation comes over his face.*) I see that you're quite busy, and I have an appointment across town in an hour. Maybe we should reschedule for later in the week.

Instead of accepting these interruptions as normal, Mr. Smithson chooses to view them as a sign that his Vietnamese counterpart is less than enthusiastic about doing business with him. If you give the impression, verbally or otherwise, that you think your time is being wasted, as Mr. Smithson does in this vignette, you could damage a relationship that was on the right track.

In some cases, you may be speaking with an individual who has considerable decision-making authority, but usually whatever is discussed will be shared later with many others within the organization as part of consensus building. Your Vietnamese counterpart will make this clear at some point so as to simplify matters should the decision be made to work together. In recent years, the entrepreneurial spirit of the market reforms has continued to resonate throughout Vietnamese society, including higher education. You may find discussions moving at a pace that was not even imaginable just a few years ago. In one instance, a foreign professor who had been introduced to a prospective partner by a sponsor met with the director of international cooperation at a national university. After a brief discussion, the director picked up the phone, called a colleague who oversees an institute, and arranged a meeting. In a cordial meeting the following morning, the institute director informed his foreign colleague in no uncertain terms that he was interested in the proposed program and could proceed without further consultation. Be prepared, though, for discussions, meetings, and plans to move slowly, with time for relationship building factored in.

In the following conversation, Mr. Chandler seems to want to force his agenda without giving Mr. Thang sufficient time for consultation with his colleagues.

Mr. Chandler: I think we've made a lot of progress. We just need to finalize the itinerary for the tour.

Mr. Thang: Yes, but this matter is a bit difficult. We need to give it some thought.

Mr. Chandler: Just let me know what dates are convenient for you. How about some time in July?

Mr. Thang: Yes, maybe . . .

Mr. Chandler: Or, we could move the program back one month. That would work for us.

Mr. Thang: Please have some tea and fruit.

Mr. Chandler: Can we at least work out a tentative schedule before we take a break?

Mr. Chandler lacks an appreciation of the decision-making process and need for consultation in Vietnam. He also repeatedly misses Mr. Thang's hints indicating the need for more time. The more you push a Vietnamese, the more he will feel suspicious and possibly alienated. Mr. Thang politely implies that it is not the timeline that is the issue but, rather, something else. He may also mean that he does not have the authority to make this decision. Typical Vietnamese behavior is to turn the conversation in a different direction when one doesn't have an answer and doesn't want to make a mistake.

As a good host, your Vietnamese counterpart will rarely initiate the conclusion of the appointment. Instead, it is expected that you, as the guest, will respect the time limit for the appointment and will signal a close of discussions. Failure to do so can embarrass your host, who may be late for another appointment, may need the room for another meeting, or may simply be uncomfortable closing discussions. If your host is glancing at his watch, it is definitely time to end the meeting, at which point it is customary for both of you to stand and shake hands.

Follow-Up

> The natural instinct is to take advantage while you're here. Demonstrate that you're intending to stay for a very long time.
>
> —Expat

> First-time visitors are graciously welcomed acquaintances; second-time visitors return as friends; third-time visitors, as old friends. Foreigners should consider managing layers of intimacy by making multiple visits that move both the relationship and project plans forward step-by-step.
>
> —Lady Borton

Remember that many appointments and meetings are necessary to keep your interests and plans on the front burner. In many cases, if you come only once and present your card, you will quickly be forgotten, or your card may be misplaced. Through repeated meetings you can ensure that your interests are kept in mind and demonstrate your seriousness and sincerity. Vietnamese officials meet a large number of foreign business-people who never return. Repeat meetings can help differentiate you from the foreigners who "talk the talk" but don't "walk the walk."

Be sure to send a follow-up letter expressing your gratitude for having the opportunity to meet with your Vietnamese potential partners. If you make any promises—for example, to send additional information or to check on a fact—keep them. Keeping promises is further evidence of your seriousness and commitment that will be appreciated and remembered. As one Vietnamese respondent put it, "Be sincere, and when you say something, mean it." I make a point of taking notes after each conversation, and, if I have promised to do or send something, I include that in my list. This is part of that web of shared favors, obligations, rights, and accountabilities referred to earlier—one of many small steps in the trust-building process. Unkept promises will undermine your relationship.

Recent improvements in Vietnam's telecommunications and information technology infrastructure make it easy to stay in touch once you return home. In addition to e-mail at work, many Vietnamese business-people, academics, government officials, and others have web-based e-mail accounts (e.g., Yahoo!, Hotmail). Remember, though, to think of long-distance communication—be it e-mail, snail mail, fax, or the occasional telephone call—as a way to maintain the relationship, *not* as a substitute for personal contact. Also, don't limit your communication to business matters—include inquiries into appropriate personal topics, such as the well-being of your potential partner and her family. Holiday cards, especially for Tet (the Lunar New Year), are de rigueur.

Plan to visit Vietnam on a regular basis and, if possible, for your counterpart or partner to visit you as well. In a country where the lines between business and personal relationships are blurred, such visits are a wise investment in long-term cooperation between individuals and organizations. It takes a long time for the Vietnamese to realize and believe that you have a long-term commitment to doing business in their country. Until that time, they will take a wait-and-see attitude and may have a tendency to keep you at a distance. You are best served by showing humility, taking a gentle approach, and displaying consistency and patience over an extended period of time.

Negotiating

In a culture that values harmony, you will do best if you work toward a deal, agreement, or arrangement that benefits both parties. One point made earlier that bears repeating here is the importance of presenting your ideas in such a way that your Vietnamese associates do not have the impression that you are trying to pressure them or gain a competitive advantage over them. One Vietnamese who has worked with foreigners for many years put it this way: "If you want your partners to be actively involved in your project, try to explain to them what the benefits are and do not try to impose your ideas, because they may think you are just interested in meeting your own needs without bringing any benefit to them, or to Vietnam."

The Vietnamese are skilled negotiators and are fully cognizant of the fact that time is on their side. They have a long history of negotiation in times of war and peace. Like other discussions, negotiations are conducted in an indirect, roundabout way, proceeding slowly but surely to the main point. There are exceptions to this negotiating style: for example, Western-educated businessmen in the south who are dealing with time-sensitive transactions (e.g., in export-oriented businesses) are likely to be more straightforward and direct.

The focus is not on people but on specific issues, and there are points at which a deal is going to happen or not. One expatriate gave this advice about positioning oneself: even if you have decision-making authority, always present yourself as just a messenger for someone else. Chances are your counterpart is in the same position. This makes for a more equal discussion during which neither side is showing any of its cards. You can be sure that there is always another authority on the Vietnamese side and that whatever is discussed will be subjected to a lengthy process of consultation.

Be patient with gaps in the conversation. These tend to be a source of discomfort for U.S. Americans and other Westerners. As a form of nonverbal communication, silence is a subtle means of expressing dissatisfaction, taking time for reflection, or simply letting your partners continue the discussion. If your partner or colleague says something that irritates or angers you, make a point of hiding your emotions. Open displays of anger undermine harmony and are perceived as a sign of weakness that could be exploited at some point in the future. Throughout the conversation, maintain a neutral expression and a pleasant demeanor, with an occasional smile.

A Vietnamese businessman with many years of foreign experience in both Asian and Western countries described the main cultural characteristics related to the negotiation style and tactics of Vietnamese versus Western businesspeople in this way:

Vietnamese	*Western*
Focus on relationships.	Focus on rules.
Legal contracts can change.	Legal contracts are binding.
Trust people, honor changing agreements.	Trust contracts or someone's word.
Relationships change.	A deal is a deal.
There are many perspectives on reality.	There is only one truth.
Take a collectivist point of view.	Take an individualist point of view.
Decisions are made by the organization or by others.	Decisions are made on the spot.
Groups achieve.	Individuals achieve.
Individuals do not reveal thoughts or feelings.	Individuals reveal thoughts and feelings both verbally and nonverbally.
May accidentally show tension in facial expressions.	Shows tension, emotions come more easily.
Emotions are held in check.	Heated, animated discussion is common.
Society is high-context.	Society is low-context.

Vietnamese	*Western*
Uncertainty avoidance is strong.	Uncertainty avoidance is weak.
Legal system is unstable, ambiguous, in flux.	Legal system is well established, transparent.

Do not be too aggressive during a negotiation. Instead, state your position clearly and firmly, but politely, with the appropriate degree of respect. Vietnamese negotiators normally treat outside information with caution, so be open and honest, explaining clearly any foreseeable problems or pitfalls. If the Vietnamese later think that you were devious or that you were withholding information, they will stonewall further negotiations. To minimize future misunderstandings, spell out terms verbally, even when a written proposal or translation has been provided. If necessary, explain your company's point of view and needs. Think of the initial negotiations as an educational process and as the first of many opportunities to become acquainted.

Keep in mind that the physical posture and reaction of your Vietnamese counterparts to your presentation may not indicate their level of interest. Following meetings, many foreign business visitors misinterpret the warmth and enthusiasm of their hosts to indicate a strong interest in the issues discussed, only to discover in subsequent meetings that the Vietnamese counterpart was simply being respectful and courteous but was not interested in the proposal.

Socializing and Gift Giving

The initial business appointment provides a chance for you and your Vietnamese counterpart to become acquainted and to lay the foundation for a productive and cooperative relationship. It is, however, only a beginning. The lunch or dinner to which your host will probably invite you, perhaps after a subsequent meeting, is a time to relax, get to know him better, and, later, to continue with your discussion.

The use of chopsticks, though not necessary, will be appreciated and admired by your hosts. It may even be a source of humor, depending on your proficiency in transporting food from the bowl to your mouth. Whether you are taking a break or are finished eating, always leave your chopsticks balanced on top of the bowl or plate, never sticking up in the bowl. The latter is reminiscent of incense sticks burned for the dead and is a sign of death. Although eating with a fork and knife is a novelty for many Vietnamese, many restaurants in Vietnam's major cities offer both options.

Because you are an honored guest, one of your hosts will probably serve you some of the best pieces of meat and vegetables. In another expression of hospitality, you will find that one of your Vietnamese colleagues keeps refilling your glass. If you are drinking beer and wish to limit your intake, take the occasional sip and drink slowly. If your glass is half empty and you look away for a moment, don't be surprised to find it full when you pick it up again. Also feel free to fill up your hosts' glasses as a sign of respect and solidarity.

Use the time you spend at a restaurant to relax and get to know your Vietnamese colleagues, not to continue a business meeting. In the following vignette, Ms. Walton, after getting off to a positive start, has gone to a restaurant with her counterpart, Ms. Huong. Ms. Walton, as you will see from her side of the conversation, is eager to continue the discussion rather than setting the business of the day aside and taking advantage of the opportunity to get to know Ms. Huong better.

> Ms. Walton: This is a wonderful restaurant. Very relaxing and beautiful! Thank you for inviting me.
>
> Ms. Huong: You're welcome. The food is delicious here. I thought I would order one of the chef's special dishes. I hope you'll like it.
>
> Ms. Walton: That sounds great.
>
> Ms. Huong: So how is your family? It's too bad they couldn't come with you. There's so much to see, and the weather is so pleasant this time of year.
>
> Ms. Walton: Oh, they're fine. Now about the program we discussed at your office . . .
>
> Ms. Huong: Here's the waiter. . . . So, what would you like to drink? Would you care for an appetizer?

Here, Ms. Walton is obviously stuck in a task-oriented mode when, in fact, she should be focused on getting to know her counterpart in a relaxed setting. As noted earlier, the Vietnamese want to get to know you before getting involved in business with you. They typically don't trust strangers except when recommended or introduced by a friend or family member. Talking about your hobbies, family, the weather, and similar topics may be time-consuming, but it is the best way to build trust with your counterpart. As noted, once you build that trust, your business will run very smoothly because your Vietnamese counterpart will be enthusiastic and will use all of her networking to make it a success. Remember, as a rule, don't discuss business at lunch or dinner unless your Vietnamese partner brings it up.

If you and your colleagues have been making progress in your meetings, be prepared to offer a toast to a successful project or relationship, or to your pleasure at being in Vietnam, and to make other glowing remarks. As at a meeting, it is your responsibility, as the guest, to announce your departure at the right time, rather than waiting for your host to do so. Whoever issued the invitation should pick up the tab. There is no such thing as "going Dutch" in Vietnam.

Like other Asian societies, Vietnam is a gift-giving culture. It is common to have small gifts to give to your hosts at the end of the final meeting, before your departure, particularly after your first trip. These gifts need not be expensive, but they should be something unique from your organization or country. Unlike U.S. Americans and other Westerners, Vietnamese do not open gifts in the presence of the giver. The reason for this is twofold: so you will not be offended if the recipient is disappointed and so that others present will not know the value of the gift.

Contracts

Phép vua thua lệ làng "Custom rules over law"

Because business in Vietnam is based on relationships, a contract has a very different meaning than it does in the West. A Vietnamese contract is viewed as a dynamic document, a foundation, and a point of departure—not as something written in blood. Although contracts may be legally enforceable in Vietnam's evolving legal system, the courts are not always impartial, and initiating legal action can have serious implications for a business relationship, especially if state-owned enterprises are involved. The main value is not in the contract but in the relationships you build One foreigner with many years of experience in Vietnam described a contract as a "flexible instrument, part of an overall, larger relationship. You should be willing to make changes as the relationship changes. Adapt instead of suing if something doesn't work." Of course, there are some deals that do have to be carefully outlined in legal form, especially with a project that allows little room for error (e.g., a power plant).

Written contracts should be drawn up only after open dialogue that culminates in consensus and agreement. As Lady Borton points out, "The glacial pace of the slower Vietnamese decision-making and contract process is a cultural tradition not likely to disappear for quite some time." Vietnamese know they lack the tools for analyzing investment proposals and are understandably cautious. A first-time visitor with a great idea should not expect to sign a contract. Relationships count, listening is more important than talking, and nothing replaces having reliable Vietnamese staff in Vietnam to move the relationship along." Don't be one of the many Westerners who misinterpret the four basic levels of agreement in Vietnamese negotiations (Borton 2001, 27).

A *memorandum of understanding* (MOU) may be a signed and stamped document that establishes legal standing, or, even though the MOU is signed and stamped, it may be only a first step indicating that a meeting took place. Western visitors have mistakenly presented MOUs to their boards in the belief that they have a deal; as many foreign business-people point out, however, MOU could also stand for "Most Often Useless." In fact, the MOU is a nonbinding document that is only the first step in putting in writing what has been discussed to date.

An *agreement in principle,* signed by middle-level leaders, indicates progress in negotiations and the beginning of an approval process. For Vietnamese, an agreement in principle takes the thinking to others for discussion and refinement. In July 1999, U.S. government officials mistakenly thought the U.S.–Vietnam Trade Agreement had been approved when the Vietnamese negotiators signed an agreement in principle. In fact, no senior Vietnamese official had yet studied the final draft document.

A *draft agreement or draft contract* is more solid and indicates agreement to consult appropriate senior leadership in preparation for drawing up a contract.

Finally, an *agreement* or *contract* is signed and sealed (stamped) by the appropriate senior officials on both sides. In Vietnam, as in many other countries, a signature on behalf of a government office or a private organization has no validity without the appropriately affixed, official, legal stamp.

As in the West, unofficial channels may be very much involved in the contract process. Vietnamese point to traffic in Hanoi and HCM City as a metaphor. People stop at the lights (official), and they also run the lights (illegal); between those limits, however, "they swerve, weave, yield, and dart in what seems like anarchy to Westerners but to Vietnamese is an organic process following the understood (unofficial) rule: 'If there's a space in the road, grab it'" (Borton 2001, 28).

Ten Principles for Working in Vietnam

> *Western management theory is based on U.S. culture. The*
> *idea of hiring the best people, paying the best salary, and*
> *letting them empower themselves doesn't work in Vietnam.*
>
> —WESTERN-EDUCATED VIETNAMESE BUSINESSMAN

This chapter concludes with a list of ten principles that can guide you in your work and relationship building in Vietnam. They were originally developed by Lady Borton but have been embraced by the majority of our expatriate and Vietnamese respondents. These are lessons learned the hard way through failed projects that resulted in losses of money, goodwill, and other forms of capital. Although these principles were originally written for nonprofit or nongovernmental organizations, they are useful in any business or professional setting.

1. *Listen, and communicate in a Vietnamese voice.* To keep your project moving successfully, you must learn to listen and read between the lines. Vietnamese dislike confrontation, embrace harmony, and work toward compromise. Any overtly negative Vietnamese reaction to a proposal is a sign of a real problem. Keep your emotions in check and avoid burning bridges. If you can't seem to find common ground, consider letting a project go by saying something like, "It seems like this just isn't the right time—maybe if we waited . . ." or "Maybe if we take a break and meet for supper . . ." The use of tentative language rather than absolutes (e.g., "Let's forget about it—there's no way this will work") leaves the door open and the topic gently but firmly on the table. A break creates time for new ideas to develop and for both sides to seek consultation.

2. *Hire the best possible Vietnamese staff.* Because expatriates, including overseas Vietnamese, may find it difficult to obtain the best deals, you would do well to hire honest, committed, and qualified Vietnamese staff. Check applicants' references carefully, and seek additional references from résumés. Examine every detail. To screen out candidates who are simply skilled at saying what they think prospective employers want to hear, ask structured interview questions with challenging, open-ended answers. This enables you gain insights into the values, traits, and abilities of the applicant.

3. *Gather and share all relevant project-planning materials.* Insist on access to relevant Vietnamese project-planning materials, including the organization's mission statement, long-range plans, comprehensive surveys, designs, maps, proposals, and plans under consideration by other partners. Learn how each project fits into the organizational or business strategy. Ignoring these steps invites overlap. The clearer the information, the clearer the expec-

tations, and the greater the chance of success. Plans change, so update this process on a regular basis. Consult widely with other organizations working in the same sector and in the same geographic area. Ask for their success stories; listen to their lessons.

4. *Require transparency in accounting and program records.* Be sure all financial expectations and responsibilities are clear, transparent, and written to avoid later claims ("But you promised . . ."). Government registration documents may require a proposed budget, which in Vietnam signals assured funds. Note any budget items that are subject to change. Set up transparent accounting systems with consecutively numbered receipts and with clear outside financial controls. Insist that all fees be overt and not hidden in envelopes.

5. *Try a pilot project.* Start with only one project, and start small. Several projects started simultaneously tend to meld: money disappears, leaving half-finished, low-quality results. Insist that one project be finished before releasing funds for another. Move to a larger format only after sharing lessons learned.

6. *Employ step-by-step stages.* Advance funds only for the first step. Do not release funds for the next step until the previous stage has been completed and monitored, all advances accounted for, and all receipts checked against current prices. Build in a final payment to be made only after the entire project has been satisfactorily completed; this retains control and helps guarantee results according to specifications.

7. *Supervise staff and monitor projects closely.* Vietnamese colleagues' friends and relatives may put intense pressure on local counterparts to have a share of project resources "slipped" to them. Rigorous monitoring protects honest Vietnamese colleagues and gives them an easy answer: "I can't. The boss checks." Similarly, transparent accounting protects honest staff members: "I can't. An auditor examines every receipt." Build monitoring into each step to prevent results that are stellar only on the surface. Use spot checks. Also be specific. If you agree on P-400 cement, require it.

If you agree on five days of training, require hard work for five days, not three days of work and two of "receptions." Here's how slippage occurs: Cement is budgeted at P-400, but P-200 is used and only half the budgeted steel reinforcing bar, while the rest is sold or "distributed." The resultant building is not only shabby but structurally unsound. Or perhaps training is budgeted for ten days, with a per diem for trainers and participants. However, the actual training lasts only five days, while the extra days' per diems, well . . . The same process applies to staff time, quantity and quality of supplies, and the like. With project partners, describe and engage in an ongoing feedback-looped monitoring process from the earliest stages of project design. Make implementation of each subsequent step (including advancement of funds) in the project's step-by-step process dependent on implementation of needed changes the monitoring reveals.

8. *Make and enforce a clear policy about commissions, kickbacks, envelopes, and gifts.* To avoid using commissions, advance funds directly to those implementing the project. Entirely eliminate paper envelopes so that any transfer of funds—given or received, large or small—is open, public, and receipted. Graciously but firmly, communicate a clear policy so that staff and partners understand that accepting such "silent fees" compromises their ability to monitor. You might consider providing supplies, training, or equipment to collegial government offices in order to increase capacity while lessening the need for silent fees. Avoid providing vehicles, which often are not used as intended. Ask that all gifts be public, small, and locally produced.

9. *Build in a local contribution.* To ensure local ownership and sustainability, require a local contribution from project partners. Depending on the project, local contributions may consist of land, locally available materials (sand, gravel, stone), unskilled labor, ongoing maintenance, training, administration, record keeping, or other in-kind contributions. Construct development projects so that beneficiaries make a contribution to the wider

community. Projects that provide benefits to leaders (lunches, "envelopes," junkets) or pay the beneficiaries to participate virtually guarantee their own demise. As soon as the funder stops paying, motivation evaporates and the project collapses.

10. *Evaluate projects.* Include formal mid-project and final outside evaluations, and make subsequent projects dependent on a satisfactory final evaluation. Funders would do well to write their own terms of reference, choose their own consultants, and require the report to come directly to them.

Let me conclude by reiterating with this essential piece of advice: doing business in Vietnam must begin with relationship building. Treat your Vietnamese counterparts as equals and prospective partners, with an eye toward developing a long-term relationship, should there be common interests, values and a successfully negotiated agreement or contract. In the West, business partners may or may not become good acquaintances or even friends; in Vietnam, such a relationship is a prerequisite for successful business relations.

Just as you would not expect your Vietnamese colleagues to act like Westerners, also do not try to be too "Vietnamese" in your behavior. This will only arouse suspicion and distrust. As with all international negotiations, regardless of the venue, make every effort to foster and maintain a spirit of respect, trust, and cooperation.

Finally, keep in mind that the Vietnamese are constantly learning about Western management styles, values, and ways of doing business, just as you are learning about theirs. A successful young Vietnamese entrepreneur observed that the most successful businesspeople in Vietnam are those who are able to blend Western management values with Vietnamese cultural values.

CHAPTER SEVEN

How the Vietnamese
See Westerners

Usually, they [foreigners] aroused feelings of admiration in us, and in a way we looked up to them as models for emulation in terms of professional knowledge and skills. In those days, when foreigners in Vietnam were a rare sight, they tended to be more polite and respectful of the local culture than many foreigners of the late 1990s and early 2000s.

Many foreigners come to Vietnam with a big ego: "I am a person from a big country. I come here to help you. I'm superior to you. You are still bad, I'll make you good." For a number of Vietnamese, they accept it even though they don't feel comfortable at all. They will never love you, they just need you. . . . Many Vietnamese people don't recognize this ego, but once they do, they will not like it and will tend to make you lose face, to fight against you in order to make you normal again. . . .

Under the influence of Hollywood movies, Vietnamese people tend to assume every foreigner has a huge bank account and money is never a problem for them. They also presume every Westerner is as good-looking and wonderful as Hollywood heroes/heroines.

This chapter presents impressions and reflections—positive, negative, and constructively critical—from Vietnamese who have worked with foreigners for many years. It is a small-scale attempt to look into the cultural mirror and raise the bar of understanding a few notches between peoples who know far too little about each other. It complements much of what appears elsewhere in this book, especially in Chapters 5 and 6.

The individuals Thai Ngoc Diep and I surveyed range in age from the mid-twenties to the late forties and come from a cross-section of professions and sectors, including public, private, domestic, and international. They have worked with U.S. Americans, Australians, Belgians, British, Canadians, French, Germans, Russians and Scandinavians, as well as many Asians. Some have worked with foreigners only since the mid-1990s, others as far back as the late 1970s. Their fields include architecture, art, construction, economic development, engineering, the hospitality industry, international trade, manufacturing, and marketing, among others. They had the option of responding in English or Vietnamese, whichever language they were more comfortable with for the interview.

Initial Impressions and Experiences

Most initial impressions of working with foreigners were quite positive, not unlike the honeymoon phase of culture shock, when everything is new and exciting. Upon reflection, however, some of the statements are cross-cultural double-edged swords. For example, the Vietnamese sometimes wonder if the friendliness of many foreigners is sincere or contrived. As another example, they may express admiration for foreigners who are willing to admit they have made a mistake, which would translate into a "loss of face" in the Vietnamese context.

The comment quoted here about ego and the tendency to make egotistical foreigners "normal" again through various forms of passive resistance, cuts to the core of the cross-cultural experience. "Normal" in this context simply means behaving in a more Vietnamese fashion. Without exception—and despite the various misunderstandings and other problems that occurred—the respondents valued the opportunity to broaden their professional and personal horizons.

The interviews reveal a deep-seated desire to learn from, get along with, and connect with their foreign colleagues. The initial impressions are generally positive, reflecting a certain openness—even, in some cases, a willingness to meet halfway, culturally speaking. Apart from the opportunity to earn a higher-than-average salary, Vietnamese who work for foreigners are attracted by the opportunity to improve their skills and for professional development.

> My first impression at the time was that they were all very open, friendly, and nice. They did not judge people by their background or appearance but by their performance.
>
> Since I was very young (eighteen) and lacked experience, I was not self-confident and was always nervous. The first time I met my manager, who was British, I was so nervous that I forgot what I needed to tell him, and even said "Hello" to him in Vietnamese. Luckily, my boss knew and understood what was happening to me. He said, "Take it easy. Don't be so nervous. I know that you are capable and will do a good job. The most important thing is to be self-confident." I always remembered his words and found out that he was right.

> Foreigners are quite friendly, even though we have never met before.

> Singaporeans are a proud lot, although some are nice and helpful. They are too comfortable with their country's successes to look beyond and appreciate other countries, especially other Asian countries that are making their own progress. Japanese bosses think female staff are more suitable for administrative and secretary jobs. German colleagues are pleasant, except one or two who can be quite arrogant. Australians make better colleagues. They are friendly, laid-back, and ready to help.

I think that I was lucky to work with foreigners right after gradu-
ating from the university because the way of thinking and working is quite different from the traditional way of Vietnamese
people at 100 percent Vietnamese companies.

It was such a fun time. I was very shy talking to foreigners, although I really wanted to ask them tons of questions. We learned
the Australian anthem and about Australian people and culture.
It wasn't enough to get a thorough understanding but good
enough to fall in love with Australia.

The memory is still fresh in my mind when I first took my job
and I learned many things. With a great deal of time and frequent
practice, I gradually acquired new knowledge, got acquainted
with my work and started to feel more confident in my field.

Likes and Dislikes

Here is a sampling of responses to an open-ended question about some of
the Vietnamese interviewees' likes and dislikes about working with foreigners. Most of the comments address work or management style. What
is most interesting and relevant to *Vietnam Today* are those observations
that lend themselves to cultural comparison and contrast, as distinct
from those that are idiosyncratic in nature and indicative of personal
preferences. The statements marked by an asterisk contain implied criticisms of Vietnamese or foreign cultural traits; these will be noted at the
end of the section. Obviously, the quality of interaction depended on the
individuals with whom the interviewees came into contact, and there are
always cultural exceptions to the rule. By the same token, there are Vietnamese who are very atypical. We have made every effort to include impressions and recollections that are representative and instructive.

Likes

- Punctuality and emphasis on effectiveness.
- They are very open-minded and accept criticism. Also, they are

very serious and punctual when working, yet very informal when talking, which makes me feel relaxed and comfortable.

- They are polite, well-mannered, sensitive to cultural differences, always seem in control of themselves, and are therefore good at handling unexpected situations.
- Their professional knowledge and skills are worth learning from.
- *Principled in business.
- Caring and enthusiastic in helping colleagues.
- Straightforward in discussion, with a cooperative attitude.
- They are very open-minded, proactive, and have a good way of working.
- Generally, they are good in the way of thinking, much more proactive than Asians. Most of the people I met are good and sincere.
- I have learned a lot from them. I like the strict discipline in working, the patience, the emphasis on working effectively.
- I have learned to consult, exchange knowledge, and work together to find solutions that are appropriate for Vietnam's policies, regulations, traditions, and customs. We are able to harmonize our styles and culture by working together.
- Most foreigners work very independently. They are open and self-confident. Some of them are extremely knowledgeable about international issues because they had the opportunity to travel to and work in different places.
- I have been able to learn modern management techniques, as well as improve my foreign language skills.
- I like their analytical ability, efficiency, organized approach to work, and independence.
- *What I like most is that they often have critical and strategic thinking, a serious working attitude, and are very open and frank when criticizing but never pick out people's past mistakes for hostile criticism.
- Sometimes, I feel better working with foreigners than with Vietnamese. I like the way of working, discussing issues openly and directly, and their enthusiasm.

- Very serious working attitude but flexible.
- Liberal working environment and equality among workers.
- I like the professional atmosphere in most foreign companies.
- Frankly speaking, working for foreigners creates more pressures than working for a Vietnamese company because you have to continuously improve yourself and work independently while assuming a lot of responsibility. But the challenges help you a lot. You end up with an open-minded way of thinking, more knowledge, and greater confidence at work and even in your life if you overcome such challenges.
- If something must be done, then it's done ASAP. For example, if after the talking, we figure out what should be done, the process moves very quickly. This "productivity" also refers to the work in general and, I think, could be the most fun part of working with foreigners. They are hardworking and responsible.
- *They're not afraid to lose face. They accept that they are wrong. They accept that they lack knowledge in some fields instead of pretending to know and trying to answer the questions.
- What I really like about working with them is the way they are independent from the common, fixed ideas of a particular group, organization, or government. For example, a foreigner protested very loudly about what was happening in his group (at an international conference). For Vietnamese people, especially when we are in a group abroad, it is very important for the leader to make sure that all of the members conform to that image—what to say, do, how to appear.
- I like their easygoing manner and the fact that they don't mix personal business with company business.

As we have seen in this section, sometimes the positive comments can also have a negative side. For example, being "principled in business" can also mean being inflexible and unwilling to consider the perspective of the local culture. Similarly, the apparently positive comment about foreigners generally not focusing on "past mistakes" is a reference to the Vietnamese reluctance to place yourself in a position of failure or "losing face," which could possibly be used against you in the future. Related to that is the reality that Vietnamese, particularly those in positions of authority, are unlikely to admit when they are wrong or when they do not know the answer to a question.

Dislikes

- Sometimes, I face difficulties working with foreigners, since they do not fully understand Vietnamese culture. We still see the distance between Vietnamese employees and foreigners.
- Sometimes they are very rude, thinking that Vietnamese (or Asians) are unintelligent or wild just because they don't understand the culture. Some are not flexible enough to adapt to the local culture and environment. They like to complain.
- Some foreigners are very arrogant. They think that they are more important than us [Vietnamese] because they have more money. They think that we will do everything they want if they pay us well, but they are wrong.
- Sometimes, they can't curb their temper, causing locals to over-react and creating negative perceptions, which makes it difficult to cooperate.
- Foreigners are highly principled in business, but sometimes they are so inflexible, for example in the field of legislation, thus affecting the result of the business.
- Some foreigners are rude, arrogant, look down on Vietnamese people, and have no respect for the local culture. An appropriate term to describe these people's mentality is "white supremacy."
- Some foreigners, with whom I worked, thought that because they came from [a] more developed country, their ideas and working styles are absolutely right without considering the local conditions and circumstances. Sometimes, they made me feel like what they had done to us was giving us favors.
- Foreigners are often straightforward, so working with them is really efficient. However, some think that they are superior; they often

impose their ideas on locals. Apart from that, working in a foreign language often creates some limitations.

- Some foreigners look down on Vietnamese, don't respect local co-workers. Some really don't understand the Vietnamese and their customs very well. When things do not go as expected, they blame the country (e.g., red tape, bureaucracy) instead of listening to locals. Red tape and stagnation are everywhere in the world, not only in developing countries.
- They are not always aware of sensitive issues, which may put them and their counterpart in a difficult situation and may ruin the working relationship.
- Sometimes they are so polite in behavior that we are not sure if they are being sincere.
- Some foreigners are overbearing, conservative, and especially don't respect Vietnamese.
- Sometimes they treat people in a [Western] style that doesn't suit Vietnamese culture.
- People who have international experience are usually pleasant to work with. They're very confident, knowledgeable and there are lots of things for me to learn. Also, they're very open-minded, which makes things so much easier. People who have less international experience, particularly the British, are less open-minded, more likely to be racist, and less interesting.
- One thing I may not like is that foreigners sometimes behave so friendly, yet keep a distance. In my country, people normally are friendly to you only when they get to know you and like you. However, this is a cultural difference, and I understand that.

Clearly, Vietnamese interviewees noticed the difference between those foreigners who have international experience and who are familiar with Vietnamese culture and those who do not. One of the common criticisms was of foreigners who come to Vietnam with cultural baggage that includes a superiority complex and a missionary spirit—the notion that they are going to bring civilization to the savages. This mentality goes hand in hand with the proclivity of some foreigners to underestimate the Vietnamese because Vietnam is a poor and developing country. Then there are those foreigners who become visibly angry and frustrated in a country where public displays of emotion are rare and are socially unacceptable. As the Vietnamese who said, "Foreigners come to Vietnam with a big ego"; they [the Vietnamese] may accept it but "they will never love you, they just need you . . . they will not like it and will tend to make you lose face, to fight against you . . ."

Common Problems

The most frequently cited problems were language, including speaking English with foreigners who are not native speakers, and general cultural differences—what one Vietnamese described as "a psychological barrier to my communication with them. Somehow, the feeling of an unbridgeable gap between us is very strong and tends to hold me back from being natural around them." There are many Vietnamese, especially young people, who have not studied abroad but who speak English and other languages with great skill. Keep in mind that though you may connect with them linguistically, on a cultural level you may be like ships passing in the night.

Poor interpreters can also prevent good communication and cause misunderstanding. One respondent recalled the time when he and his colleagues "looked at each other and laughed like hell" when the interpreter translated something into Vietnamese that was not funny at all in English.

Another common problem occurs when foreigners underestimate locals' capacity and ability, which can result in conflict and squandered goodwill. In one case, a Vietnamese who described foreigners as "very easy going and task-oriented" encountered a boss who had a tendency to micromanage her employees.

I like doing it my own way first. Of course, if anyone shows me a better way, I will follow that person's lead. But my boss just wanted everyone to do things her way no matter how inefficient it was. This led to a personality conflict. Local employees became irresponsible with their work because they could always blame the boss by saying "I did it your way."

In this case, the source of conflict was probably the manner in which the supervision was carried out. The boss was insecure, overbearing, and condescending.

Foreigners sometimes also overestimate what Vietnamese are able to do. If they always expect Vietnamese employees to have what Westerners regard as the highest standards and level of professionalism, disappointment is likely to follow. As one Vietnamese put it, "We still lack modern education and practical training and therefore there is still a problem between foreigners' expectations and what Vietnamese employees can actually do." This observation affirms the importance of training and professional development as a means rewarding good employees.

Other foreigners do not even make an attempt to understand the Vietnamese working style and do not know how to harmonize it with their own or to find a flexible way of working with the Vietnamese. They suffer from tunnel vision: they are obsessed with achieving a goal without considering their Vietnamese colleagues' reactions. In an example that spills over into the personal realm, a Vietnamese woman's grandmother died and she asked her boss for one day off to attend the funeral. Instead of expressing her sympathy and inquiring into the well-being of the family, the boss simply reminded her to deduct one day from her annual leave. This gross insensitivity is the type of cultural blunder that will not be forgotten.

The same respondent who mentioned that foreigners "think that we will do everything they want if they pay us well" told this story:

When I was working for an Arab company, my boss was an Iraqi. He was the most arrogant and unpleasant man I had ever met. He always asked me to do things that were not included in my job description. I was hired as an executive assistant but he asked me to accompany him to bars and discotheques. I refused. He said he paid me well so I had to do what he wanted. I decided to quit after one month.

This story reflects one extreme on the continuum of arrogance—the view that "money makes the world go round."

The next story, about a Vietnamese employee who worked to bridge the gap between two cultures in order to ensure a successful outcome for his company, highlights the significance of relationships in Vietnam:

Our company is a joint venture, so the relationship among joint partners is not always good. I worked as an interpreter, assistant to the general director, so I believe that I am responsible for helping the joint partners understand each other better. I tried my best to use different ways of interpreting to express the right meanings and enable them to get closer to each other. The relationship among the four joint partners in the joint venture is sometimes the relationship between contractor and potential subcontractor. But my general director did not always understand my intention, and sometimes he claimed that I did not follow his instructions. I had to explain to him that I really did follow his instructions but the way I did it was different. I wanted all the partners to understand that he was very kind to them and that if they also tried their best for better cooperation, he would look favorably on their chances to be the subcontractor. In fact, our company received a good offer from the parent company (one of the joint partners), and they treated our general director better and better. After my explanation, my general director understood, but he told me "I understand, but business is business." *For Vietnamese people, relationship is also very important and it can really help you in fact if you have good relationships.* [Emphasis added.]

Another issue that came up was rampant corruption, what one Vietnamese referred to as "the things that people here accept, though bitterly, but foreigners can't." As she put it,

> Corruption is ruining the whole country. Police get black money, the tax office wants to get money as well. In order to run your business smoothly you need to spend a lot of money to shut many mouths up, or to give lots of money under the table to open many mouths. . . . Running your own company honestly is not possible. And many foreigners as businessman cannot stand this.

In the final analysis, these practices create problems between foreigners and their Vietnamese partners, who find it difficult to explain them—or, as this respondent put it, "How can you solve a problem 'if a tall white guy keeps jumping up and down like crazy and screaming like hell that he is not gonna spend any more money on this issue'?"

Success Stories

Our respondents shared with us a number of success stories, both individual and collective. Here are a few of them:

Preserving Quality and Local Culture

This story is a classic case of Vietnamese working with foreign colleagues to convince them that are on the wrong path, a path that is doomed to failure. Ultimately, using a "seeing is believing" approach, they worked together, listened, learned, and forged a compromise that satisfied all parties. The focal point of the project, West Lake, is one of Hanoi's recreational and scenic treasures.

> I have completed many projects successfully with foreigners. However, the project I think was the most successful was planning a route from Noi Bai Airport on the outskirts of Hanoi to

Ba Dinh Square in the city with an Australian firm. At the beginning, the Australians suggested building a bridge over West Lake. This was a beautiful project but unfeasible. Many times I asked them to change the architecture but they disagreed.

Two days before our project defense before the Vietnamese government, I took them to West Lake and some places of cultural interest around the lake. There, I explained to them how much Hanoians love the lake and they don't want the lake to be changed too much. Too much construction around the lake and over the lake will make the lake as small as a pond. The Vietnamese government will definitely not like this. After that, the Australian architects realized that what I had said before is right.

Thus, we delayed our project defense and held a meeting to get opinions about the design of the project. Most of the opinions asked us to pay attention to preserving the landscape of West Lake. After that, we felt so lucky and delighted that we together came up with another technical solution while still maintaining quality and preserving the local culture.

Culturally Appropriate Supervision

In this story, the Vietnamese employee learned how to write a report that included analysis and recommendations, not just a regurgitation of the facts. Rather than berating him or criticizing him in front of his colleagues, his expatriate boss gently and subtly guided him toward this end.

I still remembered that my boss asked me to write a report on net price, transportation plans, transportation routes, and current regulations of concern to consult with our customers. First, I contacted some people and checked current regulation and then made the report, but my boss asked me to do it again with more details and more carefully. He told me, "I do not blame you, but I teach you. You should not just report what other people say, but you should analyze it and have your own opinions and comments." It was hard and stressful for me at that time, but later I learned a lot from him and improved considerably. I appreciated his support and what he taught me.

Learning by Doing

This example highlights the importance of individual initiative, a quality that was not valued under the previous economic system. Through persistence, hard work, and dedication, this Vietnamese employee achieved a measure of success both for himself and for his company.

> Marketing is a difficult job. In fact, in order to turn a potential customer into an actual customer, the marketing staff needs to have considerable knowledge about import/export procedures, tax matters, customs formalities, and transportation plan that ensure the safety of the cargo during transportation and save money. Through his knowledge and his ability to communicate, the marketing staff can persuade customers to believe in his company's services and in him.
>
> The first time doing this was confusing for me because of a lack of knowledge and experience. How should I do it? What should I do? Where do I find potential customers? I had to find all of these things out by myself. Gradually, I had contact with some potential customers and I succeeded in signing a contract with my first customers to handle their import cargo and domestic transportation. After my first success, I felt more confident in my marketing ability and I started to get more and more contracts for our company. I did not only the marketing job but also consulting and supporting to customers in different types of investment in Viet Nam with different types of enterprises, import/export, etc.

Others' Experiences and Reflections

- Locals who possess good communication skills and are knowledgeable about an industry can become an effective bridge between the two cultures and make themselves indispensable to foreigners' business.

- If your job performance is good, you can easily win the respect of foreigners. Unlike in Asian culture, where respect is based more on age and position, foreigners base their judgment of a person more on his professional ability, and occasionally on his personal integrity.
- I think one should express clearly his or her attitudes and opinions in all circumstances. When you are not happy, you should let your partners know the reason, so that both sides can avoid accumulated disagreements.
- My old jobs provided me good opportunities to work with the Vietnamese government and company; thus, I came to know both of them very well. Putting that knowledge into practice, I worked as a bridge between Vietnam and other countries.
- I am now working for an international project. In general, during the past five years working in the project, one of my successes is building a working group with members who understand each other well and who work efficiently and cooperatively.
- After talking with me, most foreigners bought some paintings in a gallery where I worked. Since I am Vietnamese and I understand other cultures well, I am a very good connection between foreigners and Vietnamese in negotiation and mediation. I often tell them about Vietnamese culture and it helps them to understand Vietnamese colleagues and to improve the working environment in the office.
- During seven years working with foreigners, I earned their respect and favor since I always completed my assignments on time and with a high level of productivity. In March 2003, I worked with the Asia Society to organize the Thirteenth Asian Corporate Conference, held in Hanoi, which had more than five hundred top executives from Dow Jones, Boeing, and other companies.
- I participated in a project dealing with HIV/AIDS awareness and protection with CARE International. Amazingly, this went rather

smoothly. No black money [bribes], no curious eyes from the government or police, no misunderstandings.

Cultural Misunderstandings

Even with good intentions and effort on both sides, the nuances of cultural differences can lead to misunderstandings, often minor but sometimes more serious. Here are some anecdotes that will help you avoid these particular faux pas. In general, be sensitive to your Vietnamese counterparts, especially their nonverbal communication. If you know the person well enough and suspect that something has gone awry or that a misunderstanding has arisen, just ask him or her in a polite and understated manner.

Communication

Each time I work with foreigners, I still feel a distance. It's not really as comfortable as working with local colleagues, and this easily results in misunderstandings. In fact, it is due in part to our innate nature. To solve this problem, we need to work and communicate more often with foreigners. In turn, foreigners working in Vietnam should understand and help us to feel more comfortable and fit in.

Besides, one of the problems of foreigners when coming to work in Viet Nam is that they often don't know Vietnamese daily communication protocols (i.e., how to address people based on age). As a result, Vietnamese often feel less respected by foreigners.

Cultural misunderstanding? A lot. First is language. Though we speak the same language, English, we don't live in the same zip code. Once, I was taken to a good restaurant in Hanoi by my American co-worker. Before we got there he told me that he had found the best restaurant in Hanoi. After dinner, he asked me what I thought of the restaurant. I said, "It's not the best." I saw the smile disappear right away from his face. I knew something was wrong but could not understand what it was and why. On the way home, I asked him what I had said wrong. He said that I told him that he took me to the worst restaurant in Hanoi. But in fact in Vietnamese we meant it was not the "*best* best," it was second best.

Once when someone let me know that he was doing something to help me on my behalf, I said, "Yes, I know, thank you" which in Vietnamese it means that I really acknowledge and appreciate it, but in fact he thought that I was ungrateful by meaning that I didn't need his help.

Many foreigners feel uncomfortable when Vietnamese people seem to care too much about what is going on with them. They ask questions, expect you to explain, even tell you to do this or not to do that, interfere to some extent in your "private space." If possible, try to take it in stride. It just means that they care about you. For example, my twenty-one-year-old Danish friend got very annoyed when her Vietnamese boss (a forty-five-year-old woman) told her to . . . go to bed early, not let strange Vietnamese guys into her house, to keep an eye on that man who called her every hour. The fact is that the Vietnamese woman considered my friend as her daughter and cared enough to give her advice.

Kissing and Touching

Kissing each other on the cheek as a greeting made me embarrassed the first time, and it took me awhile to get used to this custom.

Kiss or not kiss? The boyfriend of my female colleague started a fight with her when he saw her and a male foreigner [a colleague] exchange the most normal farewell-friendship kiss ever. Don't kiss a woman when she is not the one who makes the first intention. Don't kiss hands because it means very personal feelings.

Hugging and handshakes are very common for foreigners but not for Vietnamese. Females don't hug males except family members. Even within a family, only daughters hug their dad and grandpas. Handshakes with males are light and soft. So when I hugged or shook hands with my black friends, I did it in a Vietnamese way. Then they looked at me like I was discriminating against them because they are black.

To shake hands or not shake hands? Formal and initial handshakes are necessary, but too many handshakes, especially when you know each other pretty well, will make Vietnamese people feel uncomfortable.

Who Pays?

In my country, when we invite somebody for a drink or a meal, we pay for it. But foreigners pay separately.

Most foreigners "go Dutch" when it comes to paying a bill. But in Vietnam, it is quite rare to do that. One of my American friends was stuck in a very expensive restaurant because he did not have enough money to pay for the two girls who had dinner with him. Well, the owner of that restaurant had to tell him the way Vietnamese guys often have to do it: leave his expensive watch and go back the next day with a thicker wallet. So if you have a business meal with Vietnamese people (at your invitation), make sure you have enough money.

Telephone Etiquette

In our company, the marketing department had the job of handling calls. One day, we had a newcomer who worked as a receptionist. This was the first time that he had worked with foreigners, particularly Japanese. On that day, our Japanese general director called and he started by saying, "Hello! Kai's speaking." Immediately, our new colleague replied, "Oh. I am sorry. Mr. Kai is not in the office." Our general director repeated and repeated many times, getting louder each time, "Hello, Kai's speaking," but the Vietnamese still kept saying, "I am sorry that Mr. Kai is not in the office now," and he tried to speak more clearly and slowly. The general director became angry and had to ask his driver, who knew a little English, to speak with him. Why wasn't the newcomer able to understand such a simple sentence? Because in Vietnam people normally do not mention their name when they call before saying what they want or whom they want to talk with.

Giving Flowers

In our culture, giving flowers to each other is normal as long as you don't give roses to opposite sex, as it is considered romantic. In order to help the new expat in my office get used to his new life in Hanoi, I asked what he liked. He said he liked lotus flowers and also complained about the custom of bargaining. A few days later, I brought in some lotus flowers for him. In fact, I did not have to pay for them. The florist gave them to me for free because I was a valued customer. So I gave them to him. He wanted to reimburse me but I said I did not pay for that. He did not understand how and why I could get flowers for free, so he thought that I like him romantically. It was so awkward. It really took me awhile to explain that to him.

Praise, Saying "Thank-You"

Do this test! Show a foreigner around your house. You will notice that (s)he will repeat again and again: "Fantastic! Really great! Wonderful! Really, it's amazing! . . ." Now, show a Vietnamese person around and see how that person reacts . . . well, much less. When being offered a present, when being shown something nice, when presenting some work, foreigners tend to praise too much, which makes us wonder, "Do they really like it or not? Are they just saying it because they want to be polite? Are they fake?"

And in many cases, foreigners really do fake it. I once had an English guy keep saying the food I gave him was nice, fantastic, but left half of it in his plate. He is lucky because I am not that difficult, but if that had been my mom, she would have been very angry. Not finishing the food offered to you is bad enough, telling a lie is even worse. Vietnamese people will not mind at all if you just tell the truth. Don't play the polite game, just open your mouth and say, "Sorry, I can't take anymore food!" "Well, I don't feel like doing that now." They would just laugh and love you for that.

Hospitality

Personal caring and generosity do not always mean that we are trying to use you in some way or get something out of you. Vietnamese people, if they are comfortable enough when doing business with foreigners, may invite you to go out, go to their house, cook you dinner, or give you gifts very easily. Don't spend hours asking yourself if you should do it or not, if anything should be questioned here. . . . Just do it. If you feel you are being driven into a "trap," just be direct. "Well . . . your food is nice but your daughter is really not my type!" for example.

Advice for Foreigners

This concluding section contains advice in summary form from Vietnamese who have worked with foreigners for many years and are well acquainted with what works and what doesn't. It is an opportunity to learn in a nutshell—and in their own voices—from the mistakes of those who have come before you and, as a result, to begin to see the world through Vietnamese eyes.

Background Information and Knowledge

- You should learn in detail relevant Vietnamese law and regulations.
- Do some "homework" about Vietnam before you come to the country just to have some basic and general idea of the culture and people.
- Try to learn local customs and history. Vietnamese people are keen to learn about other cultures as well. Try to learn a few Vietnamese words, but do not think that you can perform well.

Work and Management Style

- Ask your local employees about the culture, how Vietnamese react and deal with things in different situations. They are more willing to help you learn about it, as Vietnamese are very nationalistic.
- Try to understand Vietnamese culture and education. It will help Vietnamese employees improve their skills, which in turn will make your work easier. Vietnamese are smart, keen to learn, learn very quickly and are hardworking. If Vietnamese get better education and foreigners share their experience, the country moves forward and continues to get better.
- Vietnamese often attach much importance to handshaking by both hands with bending a bit. It should not be a hard handshake.
- Have small gifts ready to offer at the first meeting. This will create a good start in working with Vietnamese partners.
- At work, be patient and be more results-oriented. Just assign us [Vietnamese employees] work and let us deal with it in the way we believe is good. If it doesn't work out, then we will learn a lesson and will need to ask you. In general, Vietnamese are eager to learn new things, but if you care more about how the work should be done than how good the result should be, Vietnamese will think that you think they are stupid.

Relationships

- Networking is very important in doing well. If you're in a network, you can get information earlier and improve your performance.

You can also expand your network with more people whose interests coincide with yours.

- You should hang out more with Vietnamese co-workers so you will learn more about various aspects in the everyday life of the Vietnamese. You will feel more accepted by the society.
- Learn in detail about Vietnamese culture and respect your local co-workers even though they are from a developing country. They have a lot of things to share with you and for you to learn. Be sociable; if possible go with your Vietnamese co-workers some day for "dog meat" and shrimp paste.
- Be flexible and patient when working with your Vietnamese counterpart.
- You should build a trusting relationship with your Vietnamese partners before you actually start conducting business.
- After your business has been done, courteous letters are necessary to maintain a good relationship.

General Dos and Don'ts

- Learn about communication style and develop an understanding of Vietnam's society before conducting your business.
- Be casual! Like other Asians, Vietnamese are often shy and nervous at first. If you are casual, you will win their hearts in no time.
- Don't expect too much; don't complain too much.
- Be flexible, charming, understanding, open, and professional.
- When talking to the elders, you should not look at their face all the time.
- Do not abuse the respect and hospitality Vietnamese people extend to foreigners. Once they have lost their good feelings and become disillusioned with Western culture and Westerners in general, it is very difficult to develop any kind of relationship.
- Be yourself, be confident, but be keen to learn new things.
- Be open-minded and ready to encounter new things. The infrastructure in Vietnam is not so good, so you should be patient. Viet-

nam is a high-context culture whereby people "talk" more through their gestures than verbal expression.

- If you are from a Western country, the best solution is not to become uncomfortable with unfamiliar things that you encounter. Newcomers have to go with the flow, getting used to new customs.
- You should learn more about Vietnamese culture, working styles, especially if you are working with government agencies.
- I think that Vietnamese people are hardworking, quick to understand, ready to study more, and open-minded. They want to improve themselves, so do not worry when you plan to invest in Vietnam. The Law on Foreign investment in Vietnam and the legal system in general have been supplemented and revised to create a favorable environment for foreign investors in Vietnam.

The experience and knowledge displayed by the respondents indicates that many of them are well on their way to becoming bicultural. These are the individuals—mainly young people—who, as one noted, will serve as bridges between Vietnam and other countries.

What they dislike the most are some foreigners' sense of superiority, lack of respect for Vietnamese culture, insensitivity toward and ignorance of customs, insincerity, unwillingness to listen, and tendency to complain. It is clear, however, that many of the respondents have developed an appreciation for some aspects of working with foreigners, including styles and traits that are new to them as well as those that are compatible with Vietnamese culture. What impresses them the most are qualities such as openness, cooperation, flexibility, patience, professionalism, sensitivity to cultural differences, and the opportunity to learn from mistakes in a culturally appropriate way. You would do well to become that type of foreigner when working in Vietnam.

Epilogue

*Money has become the most fashionable commodity
to chase. . . .*

—INGO DIRECTOR

*Life always creates difficulties. You must move forward and
not be afraid to make mistakes. But don't allow mistakes to
go on too long. And don't cover up the difficulties. . . .*

—ATTRIBUTED TO HO CHI MINH

Market Economy with a Socialist Orientation

During his November 2000 visit to Vietnam, President Bill Clinton spoke
to faculty and students at Vietnam National University (VNU) in Hanoi,
the country's oldest and most prestigious institution of higher learning. It
was a rare opportunity for a U.S. president to speak directly to the future
leaders of Vietnam without the filter of state-controlled media. Clinton's
references to the limitations of knowledge with "undue restrictions on its
use" and the importance of having the "freedom to explore, to travel, to
think, to speak, to shape decisions that affect our lives and enrich the lives
of individuals and nations" were a double-edged rhetorical sword.
Although these remarks were intended to be instructive and informative,
they were also implied criticisms of an authoritarian system that prizes
political conformity and limits freedom of the press.

This form of ideological schizophrenia, the political equivalent of wanting to "have one's cake and eat it too," is typical of a country that yearns for the wealth that a market economy can produce while being reluctant to implement the political changes that are needed to succeed in the long term. It is the push and pull of diametrically opposed forces within the CPV that—without a hint of irony—can simultaneously sing the praises of a market-oriented economy and rail against unbridled individualism. It is a transitional society in which, ironically, successful private-sector companies can be awarded the "Red Star" for distinguished achievement.

Nguyen Thanh Giang, who was imprisoned in the 1990s for his pro-democracy views and is currently under house arrest, said that Vietnam was a country rich in resources, with smart and hardworking people. "But Vietnam is behind [other countries] because the government's economic and political policies and positions are all wrong—Vietnam lacks freedom and democracy. Political reform is the key for development and stability in Vietnam," he said.

Access to Information

There is a certain irony in the presence of an adult population with a literacy rate of 94 percent within a system that places strict controls on the flow of information. Although criticism and debate are allowed in the official media, they are usually carried out within a narrowly defined frame of reference, focusing on issues of economic development, productivity, corruption, and efficiency. Of course, for those who have money, are computer-literate, and know a foreign language, access to information is much easier.

In an attempt to maintain control over the flow and exchange of information, the Ministry of Culture and Information recently instructed the People's Committees in every city and province in Vietnam to monitor all online information. This is no small task in a country with approximately five thousand Internet cafés and an estimated four million people, mostly in urban areas, who use the Internet on a regular basis. Internet café owners are required to document which websites their customers visit and for how long. They can be fined or jailed for permitting users to download or send "bad information," defined as material that is pornographic in nature, is anti-government, or reveals state secrets. All users must present ID cards so that they can be tracked down if they visit "inappropriate" sites. This is in response to the sentencing of several dissidents to long prison terms for using the Internet to criticize the government and promote political reforms.

On the other side of the coin, one national university, which has received substantial external funding to enhance its technology capability, allows students to have Internet access and to view and listen to news broadcasts from the U.K., the U.S., Germany, and many other countries, downloaded by satellite and stored in digital or analog formats. For those private individuals who can afford it, cable service that includes such familiar channels as CNN, Discovery Channel, MTV, and HBO, is available.

It wasn't that long ago that underground segments of the market economy have found a way to meet the demand for foreign publications that were not widely available in Vietnam. For example, some enterprising people earn money by finding English-language magazines such as *The New Yorker*, *Newsweek*, or *The Economist*, which hotels, businesses, and NGOs dispose of as soon as the next issue arrives. The entrepreneurs, in turn, sell these slightly dated magazines to university students and others who read English and want news, information, and perspectives that have not been screened by the authorities. Now, with the increased availability of these publications, this is as much a matter of cost as it is of access. Even government and CPV documents are for sale. You just have to know whom to ask or where to find them.

The Future

The challenge for the Vietnamese government and the CPV is how to grow the country economically without letting go of power. One Party official used the metaphor of an egg hatching: the chick is inside pecking at a very fragile shell. The only question is when the egg will hatch—in a year, a few years, twenty-five years?— and what kind of chick will emerge. One expatriate with years of Vietnam experience referred to the political system as "good in a more pure sense" but acknowledged the problem of having so few people in charge and pointed to the need to open the system up as a means of strengthening it.

A cynic would argue that those in power have successfully managed to convert political capital and power to economic power and wealth, as in China. Change means having to give up money, position, status, benefits—having to relinquish "a piece of the pie," as it were. There are many government and Party officials who are constructively critical of various policies and actions but prefer to complain in private so as not to jeopardize their position and privilege and that of their children.

Boudarel and Nguyen put it this way, sparing neither the Vietnamese government nor the international community:

> . . . no one knows what the future will bring. It largely depends on the attitude of the countries that claim to defend human rights. Will they give priority to short-term economic interests, to the construction of capitalism by a corrupt mafia that supposedly has its roots in a single-party system that claims to be building socialism? Or will they prefer to give a place to political debate that reinforces the role of economic factors in the long term? In the end, both Vietnamese and international opinions will judge by facts and not by discourse, no matter what the color of the rhetoric. (2002, 172)

There is a realization, even among insiders—maybe especially among insiders, who know the system better than anyone—that changes have to be implemented. The questions are how, how fast, and when. What model should be used? What does it really mean to have a "market economy with socialist orientation"? Vietnam's slow but sure integration into the international community is evidence that it chooses not to identify with any one system, including U.S. and European forms of capitalism and democracy.

One expatriate businessman, who is completely bicultural and bilingual, characterized this globalist position as an "escape clause" and a "safe environment" that enables Vietnam to do business with anyone. Vietnam no longer wants to be seen as a communist state; in fact, many people who hold government and other positions that require CPV membership are no longer proud to tell people that they are communists.

What weighs heavily on the minds of Vietnam's leaders, policymakers, and others, including some of the Vietnamese businesspeople we surveyed, is fear of the unknown, the pace of change, the possibility of instability, and the lingering paranoia of the war years. Given its history, it is not surprising that the Vietnamese are wary of some foreign governments, especially those that were the cause of so much suffering, destruction and death in the not-so-distant past. The sheer size of Vietnam's armed forces is evidence of the leadership's uneasiness with and uncertainty about the intentions and strategic goals of some of its neighbors. Similarly, the resources poured into the Ministry of the Interior, the state security service, is proof of its concern with its perceived enemies from within.

Robert Templer asserts that under *doi moi* "economy and society have changed radically, creating small gatherings and associations, unfocused and diverse pockets of alternative power and individual ideas that can only grow. An economy unshackled from the state has been the breeding ground of an incipient civil society." Although this may be overstating the case somewhat, there is an element of truth to it. The private sector, in whatever shape or form, is the future of Vietnam—but under the guidance of a highly centralized government and the CPV, regardless of what it ends up calling itself. The main point is that it keeps it eyes on the prize: the cherished and time-honored goals of stability and incremental change.

Implications for Westerners

How do all of the recent changes in Vietnam affect the quality of interaction between Vietnamese and Westerners who come to Vietnam to work, study, or travel? While Vietnam will remain uniquely Vietnamese, the country's integration into the international community and the global economy has created a situation that is more favorable than ever for developing relationships and "doing business." The Vietnamese are better informed about the rest of the world and more knowledgeable than ever before about various modes of behavior and ways of doing business.

What this means in a business context is that many Vietnamese, especially those who have overseas experience and/or experience working with foreigners, are often able to meet their foreign colleagues halfway and are frequently tolerant of cultural mistakes and oversights. As Vietnam opened up to the world—a political and economic necessity—Vietnamese officials and businesspeople were forced to enroll in a real-life crash course in how to deal with foreigners who saw their country as the next Asian tiger and arrived with a gold rush mentality. The Vietnamese quickly lost their innocence and have become increasingly sophisticated and savvy about the intentions of foreigners and their ability to deliver on their promises.

One of your challenges as a businessperson, development worker, teacher, traveler, tourist is to pleasantly surprise your Vietnamese colleagues and partners by demonstrating—through actions, language, and nonverbal communication—your knowledge and appreciation of their history and culture. In this way you will be able to enter into and maintain mutually beneficial, productive, and long-lasting relationships.

These relationships take time to develop, as one U.S. firm found out the hard way. This firm seemed to be well prepared for doing business in Vietnam. It had previous experience in China and hired a consultant to assist the project manager in Vietnam. But even after numerous trips to Vietnam and a budding relationship with a "good partner," the company's joint bid on a project was rejected because of "logistical errors." The company had sent its proposal to the appropriate ministry in Hanoi via international express mail. For some mysterious reason, the proposal arrived after the deadline and was disqualified.

The man who spearheaded this effort, reflecting on his company's dashed hopes, noted that "you have to know the people you are dealing with because the culture is based on who has authority and power to make decisions, you really need someone to cut to the chase in doing business there." Highlighting the importance of relationship building before doing business, he observed that "the way of doing business is by relationship, and this can be good or bad depending on who you deal with." He concluded that foreign companies that cannot provide something unique and do not have a powerful local partner end up spinning their wheels. By "powerful," of course, he meant well connected and able to keep things on track in a country in which there are countless ways to derail them and where the best laid plans can go awry.

If you plan to remain in Vietnam for an extended period of time, learn to live a double life—that of the expatriate and also that of the Vietnamese. Seek out those foreigners who know the ropes and benefit from their knowledge and experience. They know what you're going through and can empathize while also giving you sound advice. By all means avoid those expatriates who choose to remain isolated and who are sometimes bitter and negative about their experiences in Vietnam. More important, make friends with Vietnamese, who will later give you advice and insights that will help you in your personal and professional life. Also, don't expect every Vietnamese you meet to embody the traits, values, and characteristics we have described here. There are always variations on a theme, exceptions to the rule, and individuals whose behavior is decidedly "un-Vietnamese," just as there are people in Germany and the U.S. who are "un-German" and "un-American."

Be sure to take advantage of cross-cultural training that your company or organization may offer to its employees. German Technical Cooperation (GTZ), for example, publishes a monthly intercultural communication newsletter and organizes training seminars and workshops that focus on aspects of German and Vietnamese culture. This type of professional development gives you the opportunity to reflect on your experiences and acquire new knowledge and skills. Finally, view the experience as form of lifelong learning. If you are in Vietnam for the long term or acquire a lot of in-country experience, resist the temptation to assume that you're an expert and therefore have nothing more to learn.

Since you have just finished reading this book, we assume that you have at least an interest in understanding Vietnam and its people on more than a surface level. One Vietnamese with years of experience in the West noted that many foreigners make the mistake of ending their journey after the first steps. They come to Vietnam to discover an exotic country that had only heard and read about, and to satisfy their curiosity. They eat on the street, go to karaoke, see the sights. They try everything and love everything—but then they stop. They don't want to go any further, to dig deeper, to understand why the Vietnamese behave as they do, why the country is the way it is. Some even enjoy seeing how the overseas Vietnamese in their countries celebrate Tet but then have no desire to find out why they are singing so many sad songs. If they were willing to know, they would find out, for example, that the Vietnamese don't just get together to celebrate Tet but also to feel a connection to Vietnam. They would try to understand the real meaning behind the event.

It is our hope that *Vietnam Today: A Guide to a Nation at a Crossroads* has provided you with a practical and relevant introduction to Vietnamese culture and some related skills that you can put to use starting with the first day of your visit. As with every practical endeavor, there is a learning curve that begins with awareness, progresses to knowledge, and culminates in skills, as we have discussed throughout the book.

Some Final Words of Advice

> *In Vietnam, everything is possible if you know how to work in ways that are culturally appropriate. Your success depends on you—your way of working, your knowledge, your understanding, friendships that you establish with Vietnamese—not your nationality.*
>
> —Vietnamese company president

Now for some final words of sage advice for newcomers to Vietnam from those who have learned by doing. Keep these last pages handy for quick reference. They summarize many of the main points made throughout this book.

- Get to know the country and people before you come. Don't expect it to be the same as where you're coming from. Deal with the people on their own terms. Remember, it's their country—if you think you're always right, you won't do so well. (You may even be right, but that's not the point.) The Vietnamese are very proud, very nationalistic—and they will do things right in the end.

- Before you go, learn as much as you can about Vietnam from groups that specialize in cross-cultural understanding. A foundation in basic cross-cultural skills will help you learn and adapt. You will know if you're successful in Vietnam because the Vietnamese people are very generous, but honest, with their feedback. They will reward you with compliments if you show cultural sensitivity to their ways.

- Find someone you can trust, in your own country and also in Vietnam, who can be a "cultural mentor." Find an individual who can translate not just the language but the culture as well.

- Never say no. Just go slowly and learn to "read" the conversation. If you learn to be patient, you will be successful in Vietnam.

- Get out in the "real" Vietnam, away from tourist haunts. Pick up as much of the language as you can, and use it.

- Reach out, and have fun. Attempt to become immersed in the culture of Vietnam.

- Make good friends and then take advantage of their generosity to really learn about Vietnam.

- Vietnam is a good place to do business if you are sufficiently prepared, knowledgeable, culturally aware, and patient.

- Enjoy the Vietnamese sense of humor, the constant change. You never get bored. You can find something every day that amuses you.

- In addition to relying on your Vietnamese staff and friends, benefit from the knowledge and experience of other expatriates who have come before you.

- Relax. People who try to control too much (keeping a tight schedule, always having air-conditioning) will not experience nearly all of the wonder of Vietnam.

- Enjoy the camaraderie of working with Vietnamese staff—and don't let yourself feel as though everything has to happen yesterday.

- Look for the light side of a difficult situation. There is usually a joke there somewhere—learn to find the humorous side.

The prospects of achieving success for those individuals, companies, and organizations that focus on releasing the right responses, rather than sending the "right" messages, are bright indeed. In fact, you may discover many an expatriate's well-kept secret: after a period of adjustment, building a network of Vietnamese and foreign friends, and trial and error, Vietnam is an enjoyable place to work and live. The home office of one respected multinational company with a long-term Vietnam presence ranks Hanoi next to Moscow on the list of hardship posts, much to the delight of employees who work there. They earn much more yet smile to themselves because they know that in some respects Vietnam is a much more desirable, enchanting, and pleasurable place to work than even London or New York City.

To reiterate what one of our expatriate respondents advised, "Deal with the people on their own terms—it's their country. The Vietnamese are very proud and love their country—they will do things right in the end."

Henceforth our country is safe,
Our mountains and rivers begin life afresh.
Peace follows war as day follows night.
We have purged our shame for a thousand centuries,
We have regained our tranquillity for ten
Thousand generations.

—NGUYEN TRAI,

FIFTEENTH-CENTURY VIETNAMESE POET

Vietnam: A Statistical Profile

Geography

Area: 331,114 square kilometers (127, 243 square miles); equivalent in size to Ohio, Kentucky, and Tennessee combined.

Cities (2002): Hanoi (capital; population 2.842 million), Ho Chi Minh City (formerly Saigon; population 5.378 million), Hai Phong (population 1.711 million), Da Nang (population 715,000).

Terrain: Varies from mountainous to coastal delta.

Climate: Tropical monsoon.

People

Nationality: Vietnamese (noun and adjective, singular and plural).

Population (2003): 80.7 million.

Annual growth rate (2003): 1.18%.

Ethnic groups: Vietnamese (85%–90%); Chinese (3%); Hmong, Thai, Khmer, Cham, mountain groups.

Religions: Buddhism, Hoa Hao, Cao Dai, Christian (predominantly Roman Catholic, some Protestant), animism, Islam.

Languages: Vietnamese (official); English (increasingly favored as a second language); some French, Chinese, and Khmer; mountain area languages.

Health (2003): Life expectancy 65.5 years (male), 70.1 years (female).

Government

Type: Communist Party–dominated constitutional republic.

Independence: September 2, 1945.

New constitution: April 15, 1992.

Branches: Executive—president (head of state and chair of National Defense and Security Council) and prime minister (heads cabinet of ministries and commissions).

Legislative—National Assembly. Judicial—Supreme People's Court; Prosecutorial Supreme People's Procuracy.

Administrative subdivisions: 59 provinces, 5 municipalities (Can Tho, Hai Phong, Da Nang, Hanoi, Ho Chi Minh).

Political party: Communist Party of Vietnam (CPV), with over 2 million members, formerly (1951–1976) Vietnam Worker's Party, itself the successor of the Indochinese Communist Party founded in 1930.

Suffrage: Universal over 18.

Economy

GDP (2003): $39 billion.

Real growth rate (2003): 7.24%.

Per capita income (2003): $483.

Inflation rate (2003): 3%.

Natural resources: Coal, crude oil, zinc, copper, silver, gold, manganese, iron.

Agriculture and forestry (2003): 21.8% of GDP. Principal products—rice, maize, sweet potato, peanut, soya bean, cotton, coffee, cashews. Cultivated land—12.2 million hectares per year.

Land use: 21% arable; 28% forest and woodland; 51% other.

Industry and construction (2003): 40% of GDP. Principal types— mining and quarrying, manufacturing, electricity, gas, water supply, cement, phosphate, and steel.

Trade (2003): Exports—$20 billion. Principal exports— garments/textiles, crude oil, footwear, rice (second-largest exporter in world), sea products, coffee, rubber, handcrafts.

Major export partners: U.S., European Union, Japan, China, Singapore, Australia, Taiwan, and Germany. Imports—$25 billion. Principal imports—machinery, oil and gas, garment materials, iron and steel, transport-related equipment.

Major import partners: China, Japan, Singapore, Taiwan, South Korea, Hong Kong, and Thailand.

Source: U.S. Department of State (April 2004).

Historical Highlights

111 B.C.	Nam Viet is conquered by Chinese, Han Dynasty
A.D. 40–43	Revolt of the Trung sisters
43	Beginning of direct Chinese rule
938	Ngo Quyen defeats Chinese at Bach Dang
1407–1427	Ming Chinese occupation
1627	Alexandre de Rhodes arrives in Hanoi
1672	Seizure of Saigon by Nguyen forces
1771	Beginning of Tay Son Rebellion
1788	Nguyen Hue declares himself Emperor Quang Trung
1788–1802	Tay Son Dynasty
1802	Nguyen Anh defeats Tay Son forces, founds Nguyen Dynasty
1802–1945	Nguyen Dynasty
1858	French forces land at Danang
1859–1861	French defeat Nguyen forces in southern Vietnam
1911	Ho Chi Minh leaves Vietnam for Europe
1925	Formation of Revolutionary Youth League
1930	Founding of Indochinese Communist Party (ICP)
1941	ICP founds Viet Minh Front
1944–1945	Famine in northern and central Vietnam results in two million deaths
1944	Japan surrenders; Viet Minh seizes power in August Revolution, founds Democratic Republic of Viet Nam (DRV)

1946–1954	First Indochina War
1954	French defeat at Dien Bien Phu; Geneva Accords divides the country into North and South along the 17th parallel; Emperor Bao Dai appoints Ngo Dinh Diem as prime minister
1954	U.S. begins direct aid to Diem's government; Republic of Viet Nam (RVN) is created, with Diem as president
1960	National Front for the Liberation of Southern Viet Nam (NLF) is founded
1964	Gulf of Tonkin incident and presidential resolution authorizing use of force by U.S. forces in Vietnam
1965	U.S. begins bombing of DRV; first U.S. combat troops land at Danang
1968	Tet Offensive by People's Army of Viet Nam (PAVN) and NLF
1970	U.S. and RVN forces invade Cambodia
1972	PAVN Spring Offensive; Richard Nixon orders "Christmas Bombing"
1972	Paris Accords are signed; U.S. forces withdraw
1975	PAVN/NLF general offensive; fall of RVN
1976	Proclamation of the Socialist Republic of Viet Nam (SRV); Vietnam Workers' Party is renamed Viet Nam Communist Party
1976	SRV is admitted to the United Nations
1976	China terminates economic aid to Vietnam; Vietnam signs Treaty of Friendship and Cooperation with USSR; PAVN occupies Cambodia in response to Khmer Rouge attacks
1976	China invades northern Vietnam to punish the country for its invasion of Cambodia
1976	SRV promulgates new constitution emphasizing Marxism-Leninism and calling for rapid advance to socialism
1986	Sixth National Party Congress; beginning of Doi Moi, or Renovation

1991	Paris Agreement ends Vietnamese occupation of Cambodia
1994	U.S. embargo on Vietnam is lifted
1995	Diplomatic relations between the U.S. and SRV are established; Vietnam joins Association of Southeast Asian Nations (ASEAN)

Recommended Websites

Government

Communist Party of Vietnam:
www.cpv.org.vn/index_e.asp

Directorate for Standards and Quality:
www.tcvn.gov.vn/en/index.php

General Department of Vietnam Customs:
www.customs.gov.vn/

Ministry of Agriculture and Rural Development:
www.isgmard.org.vn/

Ministry of Culture and Information:
www.cinet.vnn.vn/

Ministry of Education and Training:
www.edu.net.vn/

Ministry of Finance:
www.mof.gov.vn/

Ministry of Fisheries:
www.fistenet.gov.vn/index.asp

Ministry of Foreign Affairs:
www.mofa.gov.vn/

Ministry of Planning and Investment:
www.mpi.gov.vn/

Ministry of Posts and Telematics:
www.mpt.gov.vn/

Ministry of Science and Technology:
www.moste.gov.vn/

Ministry of Trade:
www.mot.gov.vn/en/index.asp

Ministry of Transportation:
www.mt.gov.vn/

National Assembly (parliament):
www.na.gov.vn/

Vietnam Chamber of Commerce and Industry:
www.vcci.com.vn

Vietnam Railways:
www.vr.com.vn/English/index.html

Main Cities

Da Nang:
www.vnn.vn/province/danang/index.html

Hanoi:
www.thudo.gov.vn/

Ho Chi Minh City:
www.hochiminhcity.gov.vn/

Hue:
www.thuathienhue.gov.vn/

Businesses

Business Vietnam Open Market:
www.bvom.com/

Hanoi Maritime Holding Company:
www.marinahanoi.com/

Saigon Real Estate Corporation:
www.rescovn.com/

Vietnam Airlines:
www.vnpt.com.vn/

Vietnam Insurance Corporation:
www.baoviet.com.vn/

Vietnam Mobile Telecom Services Mobifone:
www.mobifone.com.vn/

Vietnam National Petroleum Corporation:
www.petrolimex.com.vn/

Vietnam Post and Telecommunications:
www.vnpt.com.vn/

Vietnam Telecom Services Company:
www.gpc.vnn.vn/

Business Associations

American Chamber of Commerce in Vietnam:
www.amchamhanoi.com

Australian Chamber of Commerce in Vietnam:
www.abgvn.com

Belgian Luxembourg Chamber of Commerce in Vietnam:
www.beluxcham.com

British Business Group Vietnam:
www.bbgv.org

European Chamber of Commerce:
www.eurochamvn.org

German Business Association (Hanoi and Ho Chi Minh City):
www.gba-vietnam.org

Hong Kong Business Association:
www.khbav.org/engindex.htm

Indian Businesss Chamber in Vietnam:
www.inchamvietnam.org

Norcham Hanoi/HCMC:
www.nordcham.org.vn

Swiss Business Association:
www.swissvietnam.com

U.S.–Vietnam Trade Council:
www.usvtc.org

Banks

Asian Commercial Bank:
www.acbbank.com.vn/

Bank for Foreign Trade of Viet Nam:
www.vietcombank.com.vn/

Bank for Investment and Development of VN:
www.bsc.com.vn/

Industrial and Commercial Bank:
www.icb.com.vn/

Stock Exchange

Ho Chi Minh City Stock Exchange Center:
www.hcmcstc.org.vn/

State Securities Commission of Viet Nam:
www.ssc.gov.vn/

Vietnam Tourism

Buffalo Tours:
www.buffalotours.com

Hidden Hanoi:
www.hiddenhanoi.com

Travel to Vietnam:
www.traveltovietnam.com/

Vietnamhotels:
www.vietnamhotels.net/

Vietnamtourism:
www.vietnamtourism.com

News

NhanDan Online (CPV):
www.nhandan.org.vn/english/today/

Vietnam Business Forum:
www.vnn.vn/chuyenmuc/vb_forum/

Vietnam Economics News:
www.vneconomy.com.vn/

VN Express:
www.vnexpress.net

Vietnam Investment Review:
www.vir.com.vn/Client/VIR/Default.asp

Vietnam Net:
www.vnn.vn/

Vietnam Net Bridge:
http://english.vietnamnet.vn

Vietnam News:
http://vietnamnews.vnagency.com.vn/

Organizations

Asia-Pacific Economic Cooperation (APEC):
www.apecsec.org.sg/

Association of Southeast Asian Nations (ASEAN):
www.aseansec.org/home.htm

United Nations Development Programme in Vietnam:
www.undp.org.vn/ehome.htm

United Nations–Vietnam:
www.un.org.vn/

U.S. Embassy in Vietnam:
http://usembassy.state.gov/vietnam/

U.S.–Indochina Educational Foundation, Inc. (USIEF):
www.usief.org/

Vietnamese Embassy in the U.S.:
www.usembassy.state.gov/

Vietnam Education Foundation:
www.vef.gov

The World Bank in Vietnam:
www.worldbank.org.vn

Universities and Colleges

The Hanoi School of Business:
www.hsb.edu.vn

Hanoi University of Foreign Studies:
www.hufs.edu.vn/english/

Culture

The Indochina Center, University of California, Berkeley:
www.ocf.berkeley.edu/~sdenney/

Vietnam: An Annotated Directory of Internet Resources:
*http://newton.uor.edu/Departments&Programs/
AsianStudiesDept/vietnam.html*

Lonely Planet Vietnam:
www.lonelyplanet.com/destinations/south_east_asia/vietnam/

Vietnamese Language and Culture at Northern Illinois University:
www.seasite.niu.edu/vietnamese/VNMainPage/vietsite/
vietsite.htm

Vietnam Online:
www.pbs.org/wgbh/amex/vietnam/

Vietnam—WWW Virtual Library:
http://coombs.anu.edu.au/WWWVL-Vietnam.html

References and
Recommended Readings

Recommended readings are indicated by an asterisk (*).

Intercultural Communication

Bennett, Milton J. 1986. "Towards Ethnorelativism: A Developmental Model of Intercultural Sensitivity." In *Education for the Intercultural Experience*, 2d ed., edited by R. Michael Paige. Yarmouth, ME: Intercultural Press.

* Ferraro, Gary P. 2002. *The Cultural Dimension of International Business*, 4th ed. Upper Saddle River, NJ: Prentice Hall.

* Hall, Edward T., and Mildred Reed Hall. 1996. *Understanding Cultural Differences: Germans, French and Americans*. Yarmouth, ME: Intercultural Press.

* Hofstede, Geert. 1991. *Cultures and Organizations: Software of the Mind*. New York: McGraw-Hill.

Peace Corps. 2002. *Culture Matters Workbook, http://www.peacecorps.gov/www/culturematters*.

Rand Corporation. 2003. *New Challenges for International Leadership: Lessons from Organizations with Global Missions*. Santa Monica, CA.

* Storti, Craig. 1994. *Cross-Cultural Dialogues: 74 Brief Encounters with Cultural Difference*. Yarmouth, ME: Intercultural Press.

Vietnamese Culture and Society

Altbach, Philip G., and Gail P. Kelly. 1984. *Education and the Colonial Experience*. New Brunswick, NJ: Transaction Books.

* Anderson, Desaix. 2002. *An American in Hanoi: America's Reconciliation with Vietnam*. New York: East Bridge.

* Borton, Lady. 1984. *Sensing the Enemy*. New York: Viking Penguin.

* Borton, Lady. 1999. *After Sorrow: An American among the Vietnamese.* New York: Viking Penguin.

* Borton, Lady. 2001. *To Be Sure . . . : Work Practices in Vietnam.* Athens: Ohio University Center for Southeast Asia Studies.

* Boudarel, Georges, and Nguyen Van Ky. 2002. *Hanoi: City of the Rising Dragon.* Lanham, MD: Rowman and Littlefield.

* Brinkley, Douglas. 2004. *Tour of Duty: John Kerry and the Vietnam War.* New York: William Morrow.

Cung Nguyen Dinh, Pham Anh Tuan, et al. 2004. *History or Policy: Why Don't Northern Provinces Grow Faster?* Hanoi: Central Institute for Economic Management and United Nations Development Programme.

Duiker, William J. 2000. *Ho Chi Minh.* New York: Hyperion.

* FitzGerald, Frances S. 2002. *Fire in the Lake.* Boston: Little, Brown.

* Florence, Mason, and Virginia Jealous. 2003. *Lonely Planet Vietnam,* 7th ed. Lonely Planet, February. Victoria, Australia.

* Greene, Graham. 1977. *The Quiet American.* New York: Viking Penguin.

Gunter, Linda Clare. 2002. "A Child, a War and Forgiveness; Adoptive Parents' Vietnam Experience Offers a Hopeful Lesson in Brotherhood." *Washington Post,* 22 January, C10.

* Hayslip, Le Ly, and Jay Wurts (contributor). 1993. *When Heaven and Earth Changed Places: A Vietnamese Woman's Journey from War to Peace.* Los Angeles, CA: NewStar Media.

* Huu Ngoc. 1996. *Sketches for a Portrait of Vietnamese Culture.* Hanoi: The Gioi Publishers.

* Jamieson, Neil L. 1995. *Understanding Vietnam.* Berkeley: University of California Press.

* Kamm, Henry. 1997. *Dragon Ascending: Vietnam and the Vietnamese.* New York: Arcade.

* Karnow, Stanley. 1983. *Vietnam: A History.* New York: Viking Press.

* Kendall, Laurel, and Nguyen Van Huy. 2003. *Vietnam: Journeys of Body, Mind, and Spirit.* Berkeley: University of California Press, May.

* Lamb, David. 2002. *Vietnam Now: A Reporter Returns.* New York: Public Affairs.

Le, Minh Ngoc and Mark A. Ashwill. 2004. "A Look at Nonpublic Higher Education in Vietnam." *http://www.lbc.edu/bc-org/avp/soe/cihe/newsletter/News36/text009.htm.*

* Marr, David G. 1995. *Vietnam 1945: The Quest for Power.* Berkeley: University of California Press.

* McAlister, John T. Jr. and Paul Mus. 1970. *The Vietnamese and Their Revolution.* New York: Harper & Row.

McLeod, Mark W., and Nguyen Thi Dieu. 2001. *Culture and Customs of Vietnam.* Culture and Customs of Asia. Westport, CT: Greenwood Press.

Nguyen Du. 1983. *The Tale of Kieu.* New Haven, CT: Yale University Press.

Pham, Andrew X. 2000. *Catfish and Mandala: A Two-Wheeled Voyage through the Landscape and Memory of Vietnam.* New York: Picador USA.

Sutherland, Claire. 2003. *GTZ in Vietnam: Intercultural Communication— Springboard for Development.* Hanoi: Deutsche Gesellschaft fuer Technische Zusammenarbeit (GTZ) GmbH.

Taylor, Keith Weller. 1983. *The Birth of Vietnam.* Berkeley: University of California Press.

* Templer, Robert. 1999. *Shadows and Wind: A View of Modern Vietnam.*, New York: Penguin Putnam.

U.S. Department of Defense. 1971. *The Pentagon Papers: The Defense Department History of United States Decisionmaking on Vietnam.* Boston: Beacon Press.

Zinn, Howard. 1999. *A People's History of the United States.* New York: Harper-Collins.

Index